Divine Love for the Soul

A Project by Patricia Iris Kerins

REBEL
MAGIC
BOOKS

REBEL
MAGIC
BOOKS

Editor's note

The authors herein write variously in American English and *English* English, and for some, English is a second language. Some learnt and some learned, to put a *u* in *neighbour* or not, and either to minimise or minimize. Some have traveled and others travelled, and so on. In editing, I've allowed the writer's own nationality of English to stand.

Contents

Foreword

"What can I do, in the midst of this pandemic, to help and serve humanity in some way?"

This was the question I asked Spirit in April 2020.

The answer came, to create a social media 'community' for those who understood the priority of connecting with Divine Love during this time, thus the *Community of Divine Love* was established.

Among many group projects and offerings that emerged, this book was an opportunity for participants to share their unique stories of Divine Love – their journeys, their discoveries, their tests, and their learning – how Divine Love and enlightenment found them and guided them to a fulfilling and healthy life. The aim is to inspire commitment to a more spiritual, loving way of life, by infusing Divine Love into one's being and life experience.

When you are positive in your words and ways, it affects everyone and everything positively. You magnetise more love to yourself and you become an inspiration for all.

Equally, when you are negative or downwardly mobile in your way of being, it affects the whole as well. In no time at all, if you are with someone like that, you feel the draining effects on your energy field.

It is the responsibility of us all to accentuate the positive in life to keep spirits high.

With this in our hearts, we need to remember that we are Divine human beings, here to love ourselves in our entirety, and then help and support others to do the same.

This pandemic has brought many together with their families and friends and yet at the same time held us apart from each other. For those who have suffered loss, we send deep love and compassion to help them heal, as we who are left walk on with hope in our hearts.

We are being called to Love!

We are being called to forgiveness! Forgiveness of all that is possible, in the past, present, and future

We are being called to evolve! Evolve into being all we can be as ***one unified force of Divine Love*** that knows no discrimination of colour, creed, sexual preference or gender.

You are being called! Are you ready to step up?

Immerse and infuse yourself in the Divine Love within this book. It will help you heal and find Oneness and Wholeness within, and bring Divine Love into your life.

Namaste.

With many blessings, Divine Love & Light,

Patricia Iris Kerins,
Divine Director and Spiritual Healer

Nicola Mackay

Dark Light

I don't know if it is the way the trees smell. Or if it is the different textures and layers of life held in the dark, green places. The curling ferns. The bark of the tree. The way the wind moves through the branches. The shift in light and sound as I step on to a muddy path, maybe covered in pine needles in various stages and colours of decomposition. But something changes within me. Something calms deep down inside me. I feel myself still, even as I walk through the green damp places of mushrooms and shadows. I crave that feeling now more than ever. It is how I come home to myself. It always has been.

For me, the woods, the trees, the mud, the rain, the dappled sunshine, the movement and creaks of ancient pines and oaks stirring around me – that is my sacred place.

I have memories of the woods from my childhood with my maternal grandmother and my paternal grandfather. They are very different kinds of memories. My grandfather would take me for walks and show me the different kinds of leaves, how nature always provided the dock leaves next to the stinging nettles. The man was kindness personified. I still miss him.

My grandmother was different. We went to the woods to escape. She would tell me stories and secrets. Pointing out fairy circles in the grass – "They must have had a party last night, can you see where they were dancing?" – telling me stories about the trolls that lived under the bridges that we had to stomp across, the water spirits that we had to leave a token for, the ghosts that lived in the old trees. It fascinated me.

She also told me bits and pieces of her life, her childhood, her mother's life, and their losses, as we walked through the woods. Maybe more than was appropriate for a little girl but I have always had one of those faces that seems to invite stories and secrets from friends and strangers.

I can feel my life woven with hers and her mother's. I didn't understand it then. I think I do now but maybe I will look back in thirty years and read this and think differently. What I think now is that it formed part of who I am and is part of the force behind why I do what I do.

I work with people, looking at who they are in the present and where they are tangled up with what happened to their family and ancestors. Uncovering and disentangling the places where they are living someone else's story instead of their own. Where they hold the pain and trauma of the unseen souls, untold secrets, and the broken promises, the unlived dreams. It is a type of therapy called Family Constellation. The invisible inheritance of our family and ancestors. I love it. And there is a deep, intimate connection with the clients I work with. But I don't do it for them. I do it for the unseen. I am drawn to the unseen souls, the missing children, the displaced, and the forgotten. For me, they stand there waiting to be seen, and as I work with my clients, as we work to disentangle them from the weight of the unseen souls, to free them to be able to live their own lives and dream their own dreams, the unseen become seen and they are freed too.

And when it gets heavy, because it does get heavy, I take it to the woods and trees. I walk in the pouring rain. And I come home to myself. I particularly love the movement from autumn to winter and the turning of the leaves. As they fall, I whisper to the unseen souls that I have been walking with throughout my week "I see you. I feel you. I let you go." The brown mulchy leaves are as beautiful as the bright green leaves dancing on the branches. They each represent different aspects of hope, joy, dreams, life, living, death, letting go, peace, and coming home to continue the cycle. As I walk, I talk to my own family and ancestors as well as those of my clients.

As far back into my childhood as I can remember, I thought of shadows and light. The heaviness of the shadows within the light. I nearly died when I was three, a bizarre and rare disease caused my blood to thicken and clot in my veins. By some miracle, a doctor specialising in that disease happened to start a rotation in the children's hospital and diagnosed me, saving my life. I remember the hospital and my mum staying with me. It must have been horrendous for her; the doctors didn't know if I would survive or not. They said "We'll know in a few weeks if she'll live or die." What a thing to have to hear. The only way my mum could cope was by telling herself, and me, that I was going to die. That does strange things to a soul.

When I came out of hospital I had to learn to walk again and coincidently so did my grandmother. I remember her saying "Let's have a bet and see who can manage first!" She was an alcoholic. She held death very closely too.

When I was a teenager, I was diagnosed with ME – myalgic encephalomyelitis. All the strength left my body and I could barely walk again. The pain was incredible. The shadows were closer than the light once more.

I had to choose to live. I had to choose to want to live. It sounds like a simple thing but it isn't. The weight of the pain in the field of influence that comes to you from your family and ancestors can consume you. It nearly consumed me.

I had a knowing of the significance of my grandmother and my great-grandmother in the weaving of the shadows and the light that played out in my life but I didn't begin to understand it until my twenties. My mum spoke often of her own grandmother, who played a significant role in raising her because of her mother's continuing dance with her own shadows. She – my grandmother – had been institutionalised several times for addiction, alcoholism, and suicide attempts.

My great-grandmother died in mysterious circumstances on the day my parents were driving up to see her to tell her my mum was pregnant with me. She was found on the beach near her house; she had drowned in a cave there. My mum named me after her. I shared that with my grandmother too.

I got my first Tarot deck when I was fourteen and learned quickly to read the stories within the stories. I danced in the edges between light and shadows with it. And then the ME hit. The weight of the shadows hit me. It isn't always easy to dance with them without being consumed by them, not when you are already carrying your own shadowed light.

I recovered in a couple of years and moved on with my life. Moved on from tarot to mediumship. From school to studying physics at university. My pull to the unseen is interwoven with a need to know how things work. All the mysteries of the world. Who says you can't be psychic and a scientist?

For me it is all about the stories. My memories of teenage years and beyond are filled with stories, some of them my own, some of them my families, but a lot of them are stories that exist outside of me. I have a habit of looking beyond whoever I am talking with to see who or what walks with them. What are their ancestors waiting to say? What words or silenced voices need to be spoken? Walking along the riverside and feeling the footsteps of the souls that walked there before. The shadow that creeps into a room, if you let it, that shows you the imprint of what it once was and who still yearns to be there. I did this before I even realised I was doing it. It was a little odd to discover that not everyone dances in those 'in between' realms. I stopped talking about it openly.

I went along to a family constellation workshop in my early twenties not knowing what it was. It blew me away. It was a ritualised form of the work, different to my own approach now. Full of ceremony and sage smoke. I was the first person she chose to work with and had no idea what to expect. I found myself standing in the middle of a circle of people representing my ancestors being asked the question "What is your pain?"

It is a very good question. Feeling into 'then' in that moment, I could feel the weight of the shadows, the secrets, the silence, the unacknowledged dead bearing down on me. I can still feel the memory of it. The anguish at the weight of the pain ripped out of me. I found myself talking about my grandmother and great-grandmother, the dance with death for both of them. And me. I hadn't thought about it consciously for years. But there it was, spilling out of me.

In the uncovering of the entangled trauma, I discovered where I had held my grandmother and great-grandmother's pain. She was married to a hard man; it wasn't an easy marriage and he also wasn't her first love. I don't know if she ever recovered from her first love. But she had a child, a daughter, to her first love. The daughter died as an infant. My great-grandmother had seven other children to my great-grandfather. One of them mysteriously disappeared in the night never to return, and this chipped away at her soul too. The loss of another child. Every one of those seven children, my grandmother being one of them, liked a drink a little too much. That is a lot of pain. It's a complex story and it's not for here. But that pain was the cost of being a woman in my maternal family.

The pull to the missing and lost children, the pull to death and the dead – it runs through my veins too. That was my 'pain' in the moment of the asking of that question. And seeing it laid out in that way – the dance with the dead between the shadows and the light – it was an awakening. It changed me. It changed what I do. It changed how I move through my world.

It wasn't all sunshine and happy days. My world turned upside down. The relationship I was in ended, meaning I had to move out of our shared home. I left my career in physics to pursue what I do now, but I was free, I felt lighter.

I began to study family constellation. I listened to the lost souls that had been walking with me for all of those years. Every family, and every life in that family, has stories hidden underneath what is known or accepted. Mine is no different. Secret families, broken promises, lost children, forgotten dead, violence, perpetration, and grief. There is also the joy, strength, bravery, and sheer audacity that waits silently to be discovered.

The dance with the shadows within the light is still there. I am immersed in it every day in the work that I do, and if I'm not careful it knocks me on my backside. Bringing in the sacred keeps me sane and keeps me on this side of the living.

I walk with the missing and the unseen, the forgotten dead, every single day. In sessions or group work, I see them first. I try to gently guide my clients to see but I can't force them to. It doesn't work that way. And when it gets a little heavy, I feel the stirring in my blood for the woods and the trees, to walk in the rain, to squelch through the mud, to lose myself in the forest until all I see is a blanket of green.

When my grandmother stopped drinking, she became very religious, swapping one addiction for another. It has been a very long time since I've stood in a church. It doesn't bring me comfort or joy.

In our recent lockdown I have ached for the forests in the North West coast of Scotland. I live near loch Lomond, and it is beautiful here, but the woods within the five mile limit of my home are not 'my' woods. We have become more intimately familiar over the last few months but it hasn't quite been the same. They are very tame and well behaved. Little paths carved through many footfalls; it takes a lot of imagination to lose yourself there. I have yearned for the wildness of an untamed forest. I have been acutely aware of the absence of it within me. The shadows have drawn closer as has the weight of the unseen.

But tonight, I had an adventure. Tonight, I went to the woods. I remembered the unseen as I walked on the old paths, I listened to the silenced voices within the woods. I found my sacred. I came home to myself. And my soul is dancing with gratitude.

Nikki lives in Scotland and is a Family & Ancestral Constellation therapist and teacher in Western Europe and the USA. In her spare time, she can either be found wandering in the woods, or in front of the fire with a glass of wine and a good book.

Deb Steele

The Rising of the Divine Feminine

I was raised in an atheist and socialist family in the 50s and 60s, though somewhat paradoxically I was also sent to Sunday School. The beautiful pictures of Jesus we were given to stick into our little books filled me with joy. And though they were secular beliefs, the values that I was raised with dovetailed perfectly with those of the spiritual paths I later found myself on.

When I was twenty-two, I gave birth to my first child and it blew away all my understanding of the world as it had been up until then. The chemistry, physics, and biology I had been taught at school, and the sociology and psychology learned at university, went nowhere to explaining the wonder and mystery of creating and birthing a new human being as I experienced it. It was too huge for my limited self to understand and it led me on a journey, to help me make sense of this expanded experience of reality.

It proved to be a rich, rewarding, and frequently challenging path for coming into deeper ownership of my own spirituality. Alongside this were my experiences of being a counsellor, psychotherapist, and counselling trainer and supervisor.

In the early 70s, when I had my son, there were few markers of the Divine Feminine. There were some feminist critiques of religion, and some explorations of experiences of the embodied divine and of being a woman in the major faiths, but even these were few. We mostly had no language for what spoke deeply to our hearts, those of us who were experiencing these embodied senses of an imminent divinity beyond theology.

Before the age of search engines and social media, arcane knowledge and wisdom was much harder to come by. Time spent in the women's movement, especially in the early 80s at Greenham Common, when there would be spontaneous actions, a sense of something co-arising, gave me a feeling of the power potential of something potently 'other' and mystical that could emerge through women connecting in conscious co-operation. But it took my receiving *darshan*[1] with Mother Meera in Germany in the early 90s for me to experience what I would call the Divine Feminine.

I had been drawn to her since reading Andrew Harvey's *Hidden Journey*[2] about his time spent as her devotee, and I travelled to see her to explore the power of her silent teachings. She lived in a small unremarkable house in the dormitory town of Thalheim in Saxony. We queued outside for entrance, then waited our turn to kneel at the mother's feet. An alert and profound stillness pervaded the room where Mother Meera sat in a wooden armchair. As I knelt at her feet, head bowed, I had a surging energy race through me saying *beloved mother I have been searching for you for so long, for so long I have been a seeker, I have searched everywhere.* As I looked up into her eyes, I heard her within, saying simply in the silence, *So? Don't take yourself so seriously, no need for urgency, it's all ok, all is well.*

---

[1] The viewing of a holy image. It is also reciprocal: seeing and being seen.
[2] 1991

In a four day visit we were allowed two darshans. On the second occasion the words that arose in me have stayed in my heart ever since, with a different resonance. *Mother, the beauty of your Love fills me in its warm embrace.*

Though there are many aspects of the Divine Feminine, and many faces and qualities given to her in different religions and spiritual traditions, that of the Divine Mother is the aspect with which I resonate most deeply, and these words speak the essence of what she brings me when I connect deeply with her, in heavenly form or as our Mother Earth.

These knowings of the Feminine Divine are often numinous, mutable, changing; and yet they are also in our blood, our bones, our ancestral DNA. As we share our stories of her with each other, in all her wonderful forms, we build cairns to mark the sacred sites we are re-membering and creating, and bring through transmissions which spark ever deeper connections to each other, to the Divine Feminine, to all that is. These are some of my stories of connection.

It is some fifteen years later and I am standing on the beach at Daymer Bay in Cornwall, late September, watching the sunset. As the sun goes down, the almost full moon rises, as though they are in choreographed movement. As a slight breeze stirs, I see that the water is rising. I am at the mouth of the estuary of the River Camel and the tide comes in in that particular way where a river meets the sea: rapidly, in swirls and eddies and strong currents. Everything is in motion, and deep in my heart and belly I experience that this is the underlying truth of the natural world. The underlying order of a life which we divide into segments, control by structure, build straight roads and high walls upon, is actually in constant flux and motion. Waxing, waning, ebbing and flowing, cycles and spirals. This is the true nature and order of life that, at an animal, creaturely, instinctive level, we know in our bodies – particularly as women, as our bodies ebb and flow, wax and wane in sync with the moon and the tides. This is where the truth of our nature resides; this is what holds, sustains, nurtures, challenges us – these sacred rhythms of our Mother Earth – the rhythms of the clouds and the skies and the stars by which for aeons we have navigated our way home. This is the Love in which we are held; this is the way that we are loved, unconditionally every day, as the sun and the moon rise and set.

Another beach, another time, on the shores of the Red Sea, at the edges of the Sinai desert. A fierce storm rages from the sea. An electric storm rages in the sky, thunder claps make the ground tremble, sheets of light across the sky illuminate the clouds and seas and sand as if it were daylight. It is magnificent! I have to use all the muscles in my body to stand upright against the wind and I am enlivened and invigorated and yet so deeply still that I feel as though I could stand here in this elemental tumult for infinity. And in this stillness, I remember that this day is *Imbolc,*[3] festival of Brigid, Celtic goddess of fire and sun.

The day before, I had been at the foot of Mount Sinai in the monastery of Saint Catherine, early Christian martyr. Within this holy place, built around the site of the burning bush from whence Yahweh spoke to Moses, there is a synagogue and a mosque – one of the few places in the world where all three branches of the Abrahamic faith co-exist in peace and

---

[3] Traditional Gaelic festival held on 1 February, marking the beginning of Irish spring.

harmony. Centuries of devotion permeate the structure of the buildings. As I sit in prayer, I feel I could sit here eternally, in this place of love and grace and veneration for the Christ/Mary consciousness. The power of this devotion, of here and now, transcends all of my doubts and difficulties with the established church and my sense of exclusion as a woman. It feels like a place of pure spirit, and the awareness of it being a man-made building, imbued with the masculine, is simply a part of the felt sense of its holiness, in such close proximity, in time and space, this experiencing of the masculine and feminine faces of God/dess in all its paradoxes. The monastery full of stillness. Quiet prayerful peace. The elemental roaring of the seas, the winds, the skies, Mother Nature. Monastic contemplation and devotion, elemental rhythms, pulses, forces. All manifestations of the divine beyond any division of masculine or feminine. The stillness and the dance.

For nearly twenty-five years, I worked within the person-centred approach as a counsellor, psychotherapist, trainer, supervisor, group facilitator. Many times, with clients or in groups, I experienced a reality that transcended the consensual norm. This story relates to a personal and professional development intensive. We spent much of the time in circle, and as we shared and interacted with each other deeply, a powerful trust developed and an opening of the communal heart space occurred, which is rarely found in a secular setting.

During this time, P had been in regular contact with his adult daughter who was having a traumatic time in her relationship with the father of her six-year old son. P had shared some of this with us, and it meant that his daughter and grandson had also been in the group 'field' with us. As we approached our final session, I mentioned that I had brought my angel cards with me and suggested we could use them as part of a closing ritual. Everyone drew a card and spoke of what the image and quality meant to them. P wanted to draw two cards and chose *Patience* and *Play* and spoke for a while about the significance these had for him.

Later, a crisis call came from P's daughter and he went to collect her and his grandson to come and stay for a while. P talked to her about the cards he had picked, and she wanted to do it with her son. Those of us who were still present sat again in circle and witnessed as P's daughter drew the card *Patience*, and her son, sitting separately, drew the card *Play*.

The realm of synchronicity, of meaningful coincidence, of grace, is available for us to access, or comes to us when we are in open-hearted relatedness. This could also be said to be the realm of the Divine Feminine, the underlying order of the natural world, of profound interconnectedness. When go into deep open-hearted connection with each other, our humanity is transparent in its inherent divinity and magic.

Circle has long been the way of indigenous people and is inherently a form of the feminine: no hierarchy, no tiers, no steps, non-linear. There are many forms of gathering to connect in circle and one is called *The Way of Council*, which draws on teachings and methods from first nation, Native American traditions. In this tradition, the speaking stick is used to hold the space for the person speaking, with different forms of circle used to facilitate communication and connection with each other, with the ancestors, and with the spirit of the Earth and all her relations.

We sit on the ground to participate, surrounding ourselves with beauty gathered from the surrounding landscapes. During the course of a weekend spent together the interconnections with all realms and each other deepen. One of the rituals we are taught in this particular training event is to walk into nature, to identify or create a gateway, and to consciously expand our awareness as we walk through it.

During the days following the retreat, I practise this as I enter an ancient deer park that I've walked in many times over the years. I feel my heart and my consciousness expand as I walk through a particular gateway between two much loved beech trees. And then I find myself walking automatically, as if I were being led, on a route that I have never taken before, or even thought to take – across the field, through the trees, to a boggy copse filled with willow and alder. As I enter the copse for the first time, I see hidden there a single ancient blasted oak, many branches lost, the remaining ones twisting and turning up to the sky. As I stand and feel her presence, I hear loudly within the word *Ysgradil*. I have no idea what that means – it sounds Welsh or Cornish and may be a place – all I know is the power and presence of this tree, which feels as though she has called me here. I approach her and lean against her trunk giving her thanks, honouring her age and beauty, saying to her the blessing that came to me as I touched an ancient Dragon Tree many years previously in the Canary Isles. *Spirit of the tree, I ask of thee, give me thy blessing, as I bless thee.*

I feel filled with the presence of this old, old being, and when I am ready to take my leave, I find a different route out of the copse. As I stand in the fringe of trees at the perimeter, I see two buzzards slowly circling overhead and I hear more words: *Woman Standing Still,* and I know this as the name that I have been given. I am transported through time, to fifteen years earlier, my first ever visit to Findhorn, when in a *Council of All Beings*, the being that came as the one for me to speak for, and from, was Rock.

Once home and able to search online, I discovered that *Ysgradil* actually seemed to be *Yggdrasil*, one of the world's *Trees of Life*, found in the creation stories of many traditions. The trunk and the branches represent the intersection of the horizontal – the temporal, human, material realm – and the vertical – the celestial, starlight heavenly realms. Each equally divine. This initiation of the name, for that is what it seemed to me, is still alive and at play in my consciousness, still teaching, still mystifying, still guiding me.

I am sitting in the shrine in the Anglican chapel in Walsingham. I'm at the back, before the wall which contains a huge icon of Mary holding the infant Jesus on her lap. On either side are ranks of shelves of votive candles, each with a named card listing those individuals and churches to whom the candles are dedicated. It was a delight the first time I sat to pray in this chapel, that the name card closest to me was that of the parish church for the girls grammar school hundreds of miles away that I attended in the sixties.

I have long had a powerful affinity with empty churches. It is as though the years of prayer and devotion are part of the air of the building. And in some, the presence of the Divine Feminine, in the form of Mary, is powerfully present. Nowhere have I felt this as strongly as I have in Walsingham.

Although this is an Anglican shrine (the Catholic one is a mile or so away), it is very 'high church'[4] – clergy in full regalia, services often conducted in Latin, complete with 'bells and smells.' Part of me feels called by the theatre of this, but my major sense is disconnection. As I sit with closed eyes, opening my heart to the beloved Mother, I can hear a priest, his gown swishing, taking a group of visitors around the wider body of the chapel. Simultaneously I hear a woman enter the shrine and begin to sweep the floor quietly around me and dust and refresh the candles. Meanwhile the cleric continues to portentously intone in the background. I am filled with the sense of this as a microcosm of the established church: the quiet background devotional, unseen, unheralded pastoral and practical care of the women, and the 'front of house' power and visibility of the predominantly male clergy (many of whom in the high church would still prefer a solely male clergy). And beyond and above it all, the transcendent power and glory of the birther of God on Earth, Mary, the Mother.

Mary is said to have promised Richeldis, the noblewoman who had a vision of Her in the eleventh century, that if she built a chapel to replicate the room of the Annunciation in Nazareth, then no pilgrim would leave without being touched by Her presence. That's been true for me every time I've visited. I feel her presence every time. And yet that feels only to be an amplification of the presence of her in my heart.

Many years ago, I learned the catechism, purely to enable me to tune into the stream of her energy in that very particular way. Hers was the energy which came through Mother Meera (which is Hindu for Mary), and hers was the prayer or affirmation that came through for me in darshan.

---

[4] Anglican in name but Catholic in ritual and practice.

Mother the beauty of your love fills me in its warm embrace. She is also the origin of the prayer I woke up with one morning, which has never left me. *Beloved Mother, let the beauty of your love fill my heart, that it may radiate with grace and humility to all beings, that we may know the truth of our own Belovedness.*

She, the divine feminine, is coming through now to so many of us in her different forms – Isis, Kuan Yin, Kali, Tara, to name but a few. And in her form as Gaia, she is both the embodiment of the earth and an immanence which resonates in our own embodiment as humans. Offering us the invitation to be and to know our fully divine wholly human selves as the co-creators of whatever mystery it is that we are birthing here now. We are blessed.

Deb lives in central England and has spent many years working as a therapist, supervisor, trainer and facilitator, mostly with women. Her experiences taught her that the healer and the seeker are both one, that giving and receiving are in truth the same, and that our divinity lies in our humanity, not in some realm beyond. Deb offers Soul Work Companionship one to one and in groups. She is also ordained as a OneSpirit InterFaith Minister.

Fiona Dilston

Threads of Healing

I've never liked to be told "No" or perhaps more accurately told I cannot do something. My education at secondary level was a bit of a mess and I ended up changing lane halfway through with a new range of subjects and a change of establishment. I had escaped the confines of home and family needs and was tucked away in a college room. I'd been told there were no rooms left but asked to go on the waiting list. This was my second chance and I dismissed the lecturer who told me I would not succeed at completing A-levels in a year. I proved him wrong.

Moving forward was not all grace, ease and flow, as complex family situations threw a few spanners in the works and I had a couple of false starts where I compromised on degree course choices which culminated in me eventually sewing for an interior designer and studying History of Modern Art part time on the course I had first wanted. In the midst of the false starts I had my first connection with the Tarot with someone giving me a short reading wherein he confirmed I'd get on the course I really wanted.

There was always a thread of positivity for me to grasp and avail myself of. The sewing work stretched me and I would spend time teaching myself skills from books. Sewing was safe and very healing for me as I recovered from the dramas of the previous false starts. I'd go into the zone and create and be able to see what I had made, which was somehow more than a grade on a piece of paper. I was creating something tangible and something that served a purpose as well.

My Venus in Virgo perfectionism was in its element as I matched patterns and piped the edges of cushions. Exploring the best ways to put in a zip, to create beauty in the utilitarian, albeit high-end utilitarian. I was safe, sewing in my garret, and maybe I should have kept it that way but I didn't.

I pushed the flow with the addition of a complex and growth filled relationship where I looked at myself long and hard. I had issues, I chose someone with issues, and I knew I had to look deeper at myself. The Tarot crept in after an event one weekend where the reader I saw told me I had the capacity to read the cards and was a healer. The funny thing was I had learned to read pictures when I had begun the History of Art journey. This was perfect as the two things complemented each other. I was happy with my new way of questioning and understanding as I dug about and explored to find out more. The Tarot sat well with my love for essential oils and homeopathy which had begun in my teens.

Repetitive strain injury or carpal tunnel syndrome? Neither were properly diagnosed or dismissed. This was my body saying "Enough." Much as I loved the sewing, my right wrist was complaining. That coupled with the lack of ease in my relationship meant that the sewing had to stop, or at least stop as full-time work. It had always been a stop gap and a way to fund my studying but had grown out of proportion and was making me stop and look at where I was at.

After many visits to the doctor seeking "something for my hand" I was offered an operation to cut the tendons in my wrist. I was in the operating theatre with a tourniquet on my arm ready for the local anaesthetic to be pumped into me when something just said "No." I sat up and was clear "I don't want this." Strangely enough when I got home, my neighbour showed me scars on both wrists from having the operation I'd just refused. She still had the symptoms and I knew I had made the right decision. I read up about remedies and tried a couple with limited results. I spoke with a Homeopath and made an appointment. My body did not like painkillers in any shape or form so it was time to get real.

Perched on a 1950s moquette sofa in a cottage with crystals on the window ledge, I shared not just my hand and wrist issues but where my head was at, and when my next menstrual period was due, amongst other current issues. She wanted a history, to know the full story, about my birth and my mum's pregnancy with me, my parents and grandparents. I found her easy to talk to and she got me. She asked me about food preferences, my sleep, did I prefer to be warm or cool, to be indoors or outdoors. I spoke without censoring, free of the constraints of the local doctors' surgery where my family were known and I feared judgement and being talked about. She could see that the carpal tunnel and repetitive strain injury were what they were but she also saw beyond that. She dug deep as she asked about what had been going on when my education had gone awry and I responded that I had chosen subjects thinking that they would be right and please my dad. I continued that my mum had died after a long illness the year before I began A-levels and that home was more complicated than I told people. That my dad was a magistrate and did not want people to think that he was failing so I was keeping it all in. My relationship too was complex and emotionally hard work but the work ethic was strong in me.

I was literally holding tight as I slept with my arms folded over my chest and my hands in fists, asthmatically holding on to the death of my mum (grief is held in the lungs I later discovered), holding it all together, keeping it all in. I'm grateful now that my dad's pride saved me from the potential slippery slope of the 1980s medical route when my mental health was somewhat sketchy.

The homeopathy helped. I stopped working full time and focussed on my degree. The relationship was in a less than good way and I reluctantly saw it was not destined to continue. I slept a lot and hung out with my cats and did some freelance sewing. I began to focus on myself.

The Tarot was my companion and guide, and my fun too. I would read with a deck of Magic Roundabout children's playing cards just for a laugh (allegedly) and flabbergasted a friend telling him that he'd had a problem which I associated with the roundabout card. His van had broken down on a roundabout that day. Ah, you could not make it up! The Tarot became my map and I used it daily. Initially I read for fun, but as time went on events conspired to make me do more. A clairvoyant not turning up at a local event resulted in me losing count of how many readings I did back to back that day as I stood in for her. Incidentally, she was the person who had told me previously I would end up "doing something with small bottles" and that it "was not easy" …hmm now was that essence making or homeopathy?

Glastonbury festival had featured in my calendar for several years and after conversations with friends I applied for and was given a worker's ticket for the healing area. I was meant to be providing counselling on the back of training I had completed but the recent death of my grandmother had left me in no space for in-depth work. I set off armed with tent, camping paraphernalia, and the trusty Tarot deck. I did not stop, I had a queue, a sea of faces when I looked up from the cards. I was in the zone and it made me, and obviously those who were telling their friends, very happy. My voice was gone by the end of the few days and I felt empowered.

I was interviewed on BBC Radio One that year and another year featured in Q magazine. The Universe was telling me that the change of career I'd read about in a horoscope had happened. Homeopathy and the essences were stalking me too, as I bought remedies and had successes with teeth-grinding toddlers and hungover friends. I loved the magic of healing with what was so small and seemingly insubstantial.

I had always loved crystals, gems, and stones since I was a child and they neatly joined my alternative family. I bought crystals every week from the market in Glastonbury where we lived when my daughter was small, carefully stashing them in her toddler shoe boxes wrapped in muslins. I was drawn to each one for a purpose, though what it appeared to be at the time was often the tip of the iceberg in terms of its later potentials.

It was when we moved to West Yorkshire that the essence-making began in earnest, expanding on the deep issues of my own life and the issues that my Tarot and counselling practice brought to me. My History of Art helped me to look at the form, colour, and shape of the crystals (I was later to learn that that was the doctrine of signatures), and from that I gained an understanding of their uses along with my ever-developing connection with spirit.

Findhorn had been on my radar for many years, having always been on the fringes of communities and when my friend bought me a bottle of Findhorn Flower Essences and then Sanctuary Essence spray, my interest was piqued and I called them up to ask for more information. As ever, the Universe conspired and I ended up on their flower essence practitioner training in May 2003.

A sense of huge belonging, connection, and rightness stayed with me that week as I deepened my connection with myself and my healing skills. I talked with like minds and it was from there that Marion Leigh's work pointed me in the direction of the Lakeland College and training as a Homeopath. I had no idea where the money was going to come from to do this or how the logistics could work but things all fell into place that summer.

Complete in a new relationship with the man I would later marry, and with new work as a medium and workshop leader, I set off to Ambleside. Charlotte Mason college was very familiar and somewhere I had dreamt of. I arrived and began another journey of learning, sifting through to find the authentic for me, whilst learning what was needed to work with the bigger and more recognised modality that is Homeopathy. I succeeded and kept going through the training, working odd hours in even odder places with some odd folk, myself included. I remained spiritually pragmatic and would often see the deeper links.

I feel a sense of achievement when I put this in words, and that I have purpose, from the girl sewing in the garret, rarely knowing or seeing where her work had gone, to knowing and seeing differences in the people I work with: the glaringly obvious when cataracts shrink and fade or someone has the courage to leave a failing relationship. The taking of opportunities when offered and just saying "Yes please" has been phenomenal for me. Working as a Homeopath, and with other amazing Homeopaths, has helped me to truly open up to giving, receiving, and believing that I can have what I need and step forward. It has been and continues to be a process, and my delight is that I can continue to grow and develop and accept myself as I work and share. My livelihood choices help me as I help others, with a very small ecological impact on the planet. I am delighted and honoured to be able to give, and have that level of understanding where life and work are not separate, where I know that as I help others to heal, I heal myself.

Fiona lives in Edinburgh, Scotland, and works online as a homeopath and therapist. In her spare time, she has a passion for mid century design and sewing dungarees.

Sue Fitzmaurice

Softness and Fire

I was born a year before my brother's first birthday. My mother had wanted me to wait so we'd have the same day. Apparently I wanted my own one and pushed my way out, and then I kept pushing for over fifty years. Hitting sixty, I've totally stopped doing that.

Religion and spirituality have been part of my life since I was small. As a very little girl, I would dream of flying around the sky with God. My brother and I went to Sunday School, and at around thirteen we were both confirmed in our church, *All Saints*. Both of us went on to serve at the altar; I enjoyed the ceremony of it all. For a few years, through my early teens, I thought I would like to join the Church and be a priest. Spirituality for me then wasn't what it is now, but God was there and very much alive to me.

All Saints is an Anglican Church; we didn't have religious icons about, and so despite the name, saints weren't part of my world and despite a firm but relatively unformed belief in God, I found it all pretty boring. I engaged very briefly with my brother's Baptist church, and I could see the attraction of the emotional highs, but all the *Praise Jesus* and *Pass the offering plate* wasn't for me.

At twenty-one, I discovered the Baha'i Faith. It was the culmination of an investigation into all the major world religions, where I'd come to the view that all had their good points and oughtn't to be considered mutually exclusive.

Around this same time, I learned *Transcendental Meditation*, beginning an engagement with consciousness that hadn't been part of my world before. I spent many weekends in retreat, taking additional courses, and advancing to the TM *Sidhi* programme.[5] This was the beginning of a spiritual life that went beyond the religious one I'd experienced in one form or another most of my life. I began to understand consciousness and experienced it in different forms and at different levels. In meditation I felt myself without boundaries, and as one and the same energy with other things around me. As I watered the garden, I was the water and the rose; as I breathed in, I was the air.

After twenty-two years, I chose to leave the Baha'i Faith; for various reasons, it was no longer a positive place to be. I spent several years in the corporate space and later left for a break, choosing to write a novel. Several non-fiction works followed, most particularly on the topic of purpose. I coached on the topic and ran courses online. As I developed more knowledge of it, I became clearer on what my own purpose was, which for several years was purpose itself. I worked with women who were becoming their new selves, after divorce, children, career burnout, and other life changes. They were hearing a call from the universe towards a new path, new meaning, new careers, and fresh purpose. It was fulfilling to be a part of supporting this creativity in their lives.

---

[5] An extension of TM that accelerates growth towards higher states of consciousness. One of the aspects of the programme is yogic flying, a technique where a mental impulse causes the body to rise.

When my children left home five years ago, I decided to travel, and these have been the years of the most growth for me, much of it extremely painful, much of it very beautiful, almost all of it unexpected. More than a few miracles occurred. By the end of 2017, I was aware that something new was coming and I had some notion that it might be huge. I'd felt a pull to some higher spiritual level, whatever that meant.

I was in south-west France in early 2018 and took a day-trip to Lourdes. I hadn't been there, and it held quite a lot of appeal. I like visiting centres of religious and spiritual significance. Lourdes became prominent in 1858 after a peasant girl, Bernadette Soubirous, claimed to have seen the Virgin Mary a total of eighteen times at the Massabielle grotto. Mary instructed Bernadette to dig in the ground at a certain spot and to drink from the small spring of water that appeared there. Soon after this, cures were reported from drinking the water, and tens of thousands have occurred in the hundred and sixty years since.

Above the main church – *the Basilica of our Lady of the Rosary* – is the *Basilique de l'Immaculée Conception*. An icon of the Madonna rests above the altar, which itself is directly above the *Grotte de Massabielle* several metres below where Bernadette received her visions. As I sat there, I felt a profound energy – it was obviously maternal, but very no-nonsense, and hugely embracing. I'd never felt anything like it before, and I wanted to stay in it forever. I bathed in that feeling that has stayed with me ever since.

I drove into Spain and heard for the first time the story of the goddess sisters Sekhmet and Hathor and understood their resemblance to Mother Mary and Mary Magdalene, and the recreation of these twin female divines across innumerable cultures and traditions throughout history. I came across a glorious cathedral dedicated to Mary in the back streets of the old town of San Sebastian, and a more purposeful mission of supporting women to tell their stories was placed before me. I went on to the exquisite mountain town of Segovia and found her again in one of Europe's largest cathedrals. I started to think I was being followed.

At Malaga Cathedral, I was told to write as though I was writing for God, and I was struck by Light and Energy from several icons and chapels.

Over several weeks through February, March, and April, I experienced the presence of women saints, goddesses, archangels, Avalonian priestesses, lights, energies, dreams laden with purple, and my connections through the ages to other women close to me. I heard untold messages from the many guides who seemed to be with me, and literally saw and felt Light touch me. I began to be drawn to examining who I was as a woman and my own particular balance of softness and fire. I was immersed in the power of the Marys and surrendered to them, to be led wherever they took me. They filled me with their powerful, feminine, healing energy, and I was aware of being cleansed of things I no longer needed.

By July I had something going on in me and I was struggling. There was an emotional vulnerability that had been brewing since the start of the Marys' pursuit of me. I felt like I was in the middle of birthing something huge – some new me – and I felt lost in it some of the time. I often didn't recognise it or myself, and there was nothing I could grasp hold of and say *That – that thing there – that's the problem* as I'd done before. It was a mystery, and I could only say that it was 'the Marys' – my euphemism now for the general Feminine

Divine – pushing something out of me I no longer needed. I felt raw and exposed and vulnerable most of the time. I was vaguely aware of very old insecurities rearing their heads – things I'd thought I'd dealt with decades before: my appearance, my weight, my hair, the clothes I wore. I lacked confidence in who and what I was. I felt clumsy, unsure of myself, even stupid. I ignored it, mainly because it made no sense. I was looking in a mirror and seeing the worst possible me. The discomfort was massive. I assumed that whatever it was would find its way up and out. There seemed little point in analysing it.

Eckhart Tolle describes this experience of being minutely and intensely caught up in feelings and memory and story as a manifestation of ego and its fear of dying. The idea of *the dark night of the soul* is where the ego is fighting its last fight before giving way to the clear light of day. Our perception of who we are gets turned upside down and every tiny and historical element of our entire inner story whizzes round in our consciousness like a never-ending round of pinball. That's what my mind felt like. What made it bizarre was it was also interspersed with many moments of exquisite joy.

As I felt nearly ready to explode with the distress, I visited the medieval church of St Mary in Totnes, in Devon. I plonked myself before a Mary chapel, and *begged* for it all to be forced through – whatever *it* was. *Open my heart,* I beseeched with every ounce of sincerity I had. I knew as I did it that it might not have been the best idea.

The next day I felt like crap. I thought my emotions were about to detonate. I sucked it up as best I could. I can barely explain the angst, the disorientation, the feeling that I was about to birth an alien through my chest wall. Every inch of me felt ugly. My filter was skew-whiff. I wasn't myself, but

I didn't know who I was. I wondered if I was going mad. The day after that, I felt even worse. I cried off and on. It felt huge. I wanted to crawl into a dark room and never come out.

When the dam broke, I cried for two days. I shut myself off. Increasingly, I didn't know who I was, and I continued to wonder if I was losing my mind. I felt completely annihilated. Any ability to function at all was purely instinctual for some weeks.

It's not easy to comprehend one's own unravelling, and I searched desperately for the meaning of it all. One after another, a myriad of friends stepped up, offering genuine understanding and kindness, and reasserting to me my own value and worthiness.

> *It is an absolute human certainty that no one can know her own beauty or perceive her own worth until it has been reflected back to her in the mirror of another loving, caring human being.*[6]

One friend, a coach, said to me: *Your job is just to connect to your own soul. Focus on the Light and only the Light – explore it – that's your one job. Don't waste time trying to figure out anything else. There is no explanation, and there is nothing you can do.*

My Mary pilgrimage continued, and I climbed the hill in Abbotsbury in Dorset to Saint Catherine's Chapel and asked her to take away my fear – and she did. I was starting to grasp the value of appealing to the Saints' intercessional power, and I began to invoke whichever female Saint or Deity might be around. I was extremely fragile, and a big part of that

---

[6] John Joseph Powell.

seemed to have to do with some re-balancing of female energies. Appealing to the Divine Feminine seemed apropos.

I went to France, to a whole series of new and powerful places. The messages I received from each were forceful and instructive. Every one of them had to do with love.

At Vézelay, I felt whole for the first time in months – light, and with a full and open heart. I went to the crypt of the *Abbaye Sainte-Marie-Madeleine* where Mary Magdalene's relics rest and sat there for several hours. I felt a golden beam of light run through the crypt, from the crucifix at one end to the Magdalene's relics at the other.

In the hills north-east of Marseilles, I sat in the *Grotte de la Sainte-Baume*, where legend says Mary Magdalene lived. I knew I had been here before. Everything about it seemed familiar.

At Rocamadour, I had a beautiful experience in one of the several chapels. I suddenly had so much love for myself. I thought *So this is what that's supposed to feel like!* It made me wonder if I'd ever loved myself before. There was a clear instruction to love the God that was within me, because that *was* me. I was joyful.

At the *Basilique de Sainte-Anne-d'Auray* in Brittany, I sat in the presence of Saint Anne, the grandmother of all grandmothers. Not quite the same no-nonsense maternal of Lourdes, it was complete acceptance and utter safety.

These experiences are very simple and clear. They are some pure and ultimate expression. I'm sure there are other sacred places in the world where one can experience the 'maternal, embracing, and no-nonsense' of Lourdes just as powerfully, but probably not *more* powerfully. The experience of Mary the Mother is the experience of the most divine expression of these things. Mary is a gateway to them – not the only gateway, but a significant one. It is the feminine energies that open our heart, and it is in the opening of our heart that we grow and expand, connect more readily to the Divine, and thus to our purpose and its unfolding.

One of the great gifts of these many sainted women is the reality of the shame they resisted as opposed to that imposed on them and given to us in the traditional (ie. patriarchal) stories we're told of them. Mary Magdalene, branded for most of history as a prostitute. What a difference it might have made to all of us had the western world been raised on a steady diet of women who in actuality had rejected shame.

Some days my own shame threatened to overwhelm me. It was only as I came to what was ultimately its nadir that I realised the extent and seriousness of it. It didn't relate to anything in particular – it was an accumulation, both from my own life and seemingly from the lives of women before me; it was in my DNA.

There were more months of up and down. In India, the message finally came: *Stop pushing.* Which shone a light on my entire existence. On and off through my adult life, I've raged, bemoaned, grieved, despaired, and immersed myself in a long list of pains I believed were inflicted on me by others – lovers, friends, employers, fathers, brothers, sisters – waiting for apologies, resolution, or someone's return to my life. I wanted to know why. Why had those things happened? Why was that person so cruel? Why did they do that to me? Aren't I a good person?

Shame sloughed off, bit by bit. Calm like no other descended. Light shone, lighter and clearer than ever. And I was that Light. Power – a different power – became who I was.

There weren't answers to the *whys*. There didn't need to be. I could choose immersion in the pain or the light. It was that simple. Pain didn't have to be got rid of – perhaps *couldn't* be – but I didn't have to inhabit it.

Without *the Marys*, I would not have taken this crucial journey through and beyond my own shame, my darkness, my shadow. I was hit so hard that I had no choice but to surrender.

I emerged into softness and fire. Stripped bare by *the Marys*, but held in the collective palms of their hands throughout, I fell into my own darkness, eventually accepting it, and with that it turned into light. Everything in my life now vibrates with the power of the Divine Feminine – the people I meet, the places I go, the work I do, the clients that come my way, the projects and ideas that flow through me. The masculine was always there, albeit not always divinely so, but I was disconnected from the feminine. As she blossoms and emerges within me, the masculine around me is allowed now to just *be*. I don't need to fight anymore, least of all myself.

Sue lives in Wellington, New Zealand, although she's spent most of the last five years travelling the Celtic world and meeting as many dogs as possible. She's an author, editor, publisher, avid seeker, finder, and proud Kiwi.

Roslyn Strom

Chrysalis of Trauma and Faith

Four words through the phone and my world warped. Staring through the glass of my parents' screen door, the bees hung suspended in air. I could see each feather outlined on a jay's wing as it landed in the crabapple tree in front of me, its dark probing eye staring back at me, pushing my amygdala, the portion of my brain creating this flexation in relativity, to critical mass.

One of my hardest lessons began. No matter how much you plead, time plows right over you. How your brain reacts is of little consequence on a spinning mass hurtling through space.

I knew even before I was told. I asked what hospital he was in and two words broke me. I had been meeting the gaze of a bird and was now somehow staring at closet doors with my ass on the floor. This piercing sound forcing me to cover my ears that apparently was coming from me.

I needed to dart, flee like prey. A survival portion of my brain still running the show and shoving me along the flight or fight pathway. I dodged through parents, pushing away hands that tried touch me. I learned when in abject grief or severe pain, my brain does not want anyone to touch me for any reason.

I grabbed my car keys and they were wrestled from me. I needed to vomit. I had no clue what was going on. Who vomits after finding out these things? Who refuses to be hugged or wants to run from those around them? What was wrong with me? This isn't how people are supposed to respond to death. I had not read about this in novels or watched it in movies. Women always eventually want to be hugged and consoled. They don't puke.

What I didn't know then is stress hormones were still flooding my brain and body. They impact so many systems, including the digestive system.

I had weathered so much in my twenty-four years on the planet. My life was not a pissing contest. I knew that many people in the world had lives that were short, brutal, filled with neglect and atrocities. I knew to be grateful for what options I had and for my future.

I had been diligent with my religion. I had kept faith through so many obstacles, so many questions. This was not the first death I had experienced. This was the death that broke me in every way possible, including my faith.

As a small child, I had found escape and comfort in Sunday school. My grandmother was overbearing when it came to religion. My mother and father were relaxed about the topic to the point it was rarely discussed at home, just that the children needed to go to church. I had been the only one christened as an infant, and I am certain this was meddling from grandmother. My mother wasn't that interested in church but for some reason it was crucial that my siblings and I go for at least a few years as small children. I am sure that was my grandmother pressuring my mom, who at least made some friends in the congregation.

I had the unfortunate luck of being a focus and project of my mom's sister. To this day, discussions with her daughters have never explained the twisted fixation she had with me, long into my late twenties. She was highly competitive with my mother; the sisters were pitted against each other by my grandmother. I was my mother's sole daughter, so that may have played into my aunt's need to target and tear down a young girl.

Between my mother not defending me or joining in, my grandmother's stinging scrutiny, and my aunt's hateful rhetoric, I was on my own and unprotected from adults before I was five years old.

Sunday school provided a place that said I was loved and had value. I am sure that is how I fell in love with the songs and trappings of church.

My aunt, who was extremely religious, noticed I enjoyed church, a different church than *her* church. She pulled me aside when my mother was out of earshot to make sure I knew that *I was too ugly to go to heaven and Jesus would never want me.*

I was crushed the first time she told me this. Being rejected by Jesus was so hard on my kindergarten heart. I kept going to church though, despite hearing this nearly weekly from my aunt. I began to accept the idea I was going to go to hell, but I still went to church anyway.

The strange thing is I never had any teachings of division between people, between women and men, or that a person's worth was based on looks, materials, or fire and brimstone, not from my actual pastor nor my Sunday School teacher.

Where I was taught that I personally was going to hell, and that you could go to hell by going to the wrong building, was from my relatives. My grandmother, aunt, and her son, drilled in the old testament punishment and worthlessness that was used to control people.

The dichotomies messed with my head. We all attended different Protestant churches. The *green church* I grew up in was three blocks down the same street from the *white painted church* my aunt and her family attended.

Somehow, all the people in the green church were destined for hell. Same religion, same denomination, with one using more Old Testament and one more New Testament. Three blocks separated people who were going to hell. Don't even mention the Catholics in a nearby town, they were going to a special hell.

I was a small child and it was idiotic that people could all believe in the same God, but different buildings were going to hell. I was going to hell either way, but that didn't mean others were.

My mom never discussed these things. Our church never mentioned hell and certainly not who was going there, particularly children. My aunt used religion as weapon against me, a way to damage a child.

I didn't pray correctly to her standards and was chastised publicly in a girls bible study group she ran when I was a teen. I was the group example of how to do everything wrong. When I became the group example of how to end up in hell, I quit her group.

I was a good kid, excelled in school and was never in trouble. My home life was filled with chaos, misogyny, verbal and physical abuse. I tried very hard be perfect in school because

I was judged so harshly by my mother over my body and any possible flaw.

My aunt's son was several years older than me and ran a combined youth group for both churches. I was treated like I had crossed into enemy lines.

His teaching one afternoon was on the obedience and servitude women should have to men. My hackles were instantly up. I had three younger brothers. One was eighteen months younger and was my bully at school as well as home. And my dad acted like I only existed for household chores.

When I disagreed with my cousin that women must obey men because they were made from Adam's rib, he was livid. How dare a younger female question his authority? But there was no way I was going to obey him just because of his anatomy. That was Old Testament nonsense.

He threatened to tell his mother. I burst out laughing before leaving him sputtering in the church. I had a mile walk home, but I felt so much lighter.

I started reading the teachings on various religions from the school library. I was very interested in books on Confucius and Taoism. I had read *Origin of Species* at thirteen and fully embraced evolution and science.

I had never had issues with other religions. The idea that people with other beliefs or no beliefs were destined for hell made as much sense as two buildings practicing the same religion three blocks apart, but one would arbitrarily destined for hell. I didn't buy into it, but I still believed I was going to hell no matter how good I tried to be. I had been broken down in so many ways from such an early age that I didn't question it. I believed there was something wrong with me and that that was the reason for all the abuse and neglect that had started during my formative years, something my other siblings did not experience to the same degree and can never understand.

Growing up in the church, I thought spirituality and faith were interchangeable terms. I still had faith, despite all these obstacles and not being able to make sense of what I saw happening in the world at the time with a loving God. Apartheid, Mandela in prison, the Cold War, whales on the brink of extinction, the famines that were going on, so many people dying after short, brutal lives. Redirecting my mother's anger from my two year old brother onto myself so I would be beat instead. That's what killed my heart the most. I loved my youngest brothers so much. I defended them and protected them like a bear from our own mother. No loving god could let this happen to perfectly innocent souls. They were too young to have done anything.

That was when I started to lose faith. I was still a spiritual person, but I had spent too much of my life praying and pleading, trying to be better, convinced if I could do everything just right and have enough devotion that things would be better.

It was the desperation of a teen trying to fix chaos through faith. I wish someone had explained it doesn't work that way. I had been betrayed on so many different fronts, the final betrayal was the hardest.

I had made it to grad school. I still clung to faith, although I believed I had sealed my destiny with hell with several suicide attempts. Attempts are never cries for help, let's be clear. I was so lucky I had a stubborn little voice that would surface after I had overdosed. It would list the reasons I should call the ambulance or try to get to the ER. I just wanted out. I had lost the battle and could not fight anymore.

I would eventually pay attention to what was being said. I never told my family and did not have them contacted. Definitely not cries for help.

Fractured, faltering faith, but I still had an innate need for spirituality in my life. I went to every church in my college town. Nothing resonated or fit where I was in life.

When his death occurred, that was my final betrayal. People turn to their faith during these times. Every time I heard *he's in a better place,* I was livid. I must be a horrible, selfish person. I wanted him *here.* I found none of the comfort that others apparently found.

I knew the first thing I would be told is my faith was not strong enough. I had struggled and dealt with so many obstacles in the construct of this religion my relatives bound me in. I was done.

It was freeing and shocking to say I was an atheist. I truly believed there was nothing else, even while I grieved heavily. I had to withdraw from classes. I saw a therapist, but the grief was devastating. This man I had known since childhood, he was everything and my kryptonite, even though I declined his proposal two years before.

I was expected to just get over it. Grief doesn't work that way. I knew I was circling through the different stages. I no longer had a religion to hold onto, no faith in anything. My belief in spirituality had waned.

I was on the floor, listening to music he would always play for me. Scents are etched in our memories. To this day, despite other relationships, I would recognize the smell of this man. He smelled best to me when he came in from working on his motorbike.: sweat, oil and some grease from the bike. That smell was hardwired after years.

While lying there clutching a pillow, thinking about what I was going to do now that there really was nothing left and religion was a crock, I was surrounded by a warmth and the smell of him from working on his bike. My pillow smelled like him. I thought I had lost my mind.

For days my pillow smelled like him and I questioned being an atheist. I didn't believe in the Christian God construct anymore, but it didn't mean I wasn't still a spiritual person. I had lost faith. I learned that religion, faith, and spirituality are not interchangeable words.

It was a very confusing path I ended up on. I accidentally ended up in my first Reiki attunement. It was an odd experience.

We went through teachings for each level and each attunement left me fried and loopy. During that four day weekend, we all went through to the Master Reiki level attunement.

Six months later, the group of us were asked to come to Arizona, where our Reiki master lived. She said that if we enjoyed the Reiki attunements, we should really try an empowerment. We didn't know what that was, but thought it would be fun to see each other again. The Reiki attunements had been strange for some of us, but we were all game to try an empowerment.

When we arrived, she showed us a Medicine Buddha and said we would have a teaching from a Buddhist Rinpoche the next day. The experience was like being tossed out of a boat as a way to learn to swim.

It took me a while to figure out exactly where I belonged. In Tibetan Buddhism, they talk about the hook and the eye. I did a lot of studying. I found it quite funny I was attracted to a religion that had so many different hells.

At my local used book store, they had a surprisingly large collection on Tibetan Buddhism. I flicked through and the cover of a book froze me. There was no title, only the face of an aged Rinpoche. I did not know who he was, but I knew he was extremely important to me. His image swelled my heart and brought tears to my eyes.

I bought the book, read it, did some research to find that he was one of the first Rinpoches to ordain female Lamas, one who taught only an hour away from me.

The first time I went to the Gompa, I knew I had found and heard the melody sung by this Lama. This school, this Lama, this Rinpoche, this was home.

My spirituality grew. My faith grew. The religion is a way to work on myself, on my own flaws, on my own nature. My Lama helped me to stop punishing myself. She approaches me sometimes like she's holding out seeds for a bird that might flit away. She understands more about me than I do, and can be quite firm when needed.

I fall and I get up. I no longer hope something else will help me fix a situation. Grief is different now; I do not have a bargaining stage. I believe in reincarnation but still waver and think about him being 'up there.'

I think it works out based on your own beliefs. No one is right or wrong. No one has a place to judge a person's beliefs unless they are harmful to another human being. That is not the basis of bettering yourself and taking care of others.

The particular religion I practice gives me the parameters to keep faith in compassion and keeps my spirituality alight. That can be any form of practice or approach for anyone.

I am far from perfect, my practice always needs work, but I keep trying. I found a place where I am safe.

Roslyn lives in Washington state. She enjoys training dogs using positive reinforcement, has delved into the world of scent work over the past year with her current Service Dog, Bo Peep. She enjoys volunteering (pre-Covid), loves the outdoors, snow, growing exotic succulents and discovering her voice.

Dianne Graham

Finding My Voice

I was born Dianne Kape. Kape is a Maori name. Dad's mum had come out to New Zealand on a nursing ship in 1915. She married a part-Maori man, Jack Lewis Kape, and Dad was their second child of five. Nana was ashamed of 'having' to marry and would have preferred to marry a white man, and I sensed her powerlessness in this. I recall her using the word 'nigger' often when referring to Maori. Pop was shamed for being of colour and it was never talked about. Our name was usually pronounced the English way, Cappy, rather than the Maori 'Kar-pe' (the 'e' as in pet). It wasn't until I was in my mid-forties that I found out the name had been shortened five generations back by English-speaking people who couldn't pronounce Kaperiere, which means Gabriel, taken from the early missionary teachings, as Gabriel had appeared in a vision to one of my ancestors. Maori culture was looked down on and schools forbade the language being spoken.

Around my twelfth year, Mum insisted I do confirmation lessons and be confirmed in the Lutheran church. All twelve year olds are becoming aware of where babies come from and I asked the pastor "If Mary was a virgin, how did she get pregnant with Jesus?" He turned pink, stuttered a few times, and said "It was a miracle and you just have to accept that." I'd wanted some glorious answer so any vague interest in Jesus dissolved about then. Some Hare Krishnas had been handing out pamphlets and singing in town. They were far more interesting, as was a book on the basics of Buddhism a friend lent me.

I worked as a telecommunications technician with the Post Office. Telecommunications in the early seventies was reliant on crystal radio sets. Six months of my engineering studies was about the ability of crystals – in particular clear quartz and rose quartz – to transmit and translate pure frequencies. Here's where my love and appreciation of crystals began. Knowing the science of them, I know the healing gifts they bring to our world. It's also where I learned that every single object has a measurable energy, and so I understood the world in a language of frequency.

At twenty-three I married a man a lot like my dad, emotionally (although not physically) abusive. I didn't see it at the time though. When he proposed to me, I'd thought 'I'd better grab this. No-one else will ever want me.' I gave birth to a daughter when I was twenty-seven and a son when I was twenty-nine. I experienced severe post-natal depression after both births and struggled to get through days. I wasn't in paid employment any longer and all sense of purpose or belonging disappeared. I felt powerless.

After our daughter's birth there was some pressure from his family to have her christened. I wasn't keen on the idea and preferred the idea of children being dedicated to God and being able to decide at a later age if they wanted to be christened. Nonetheless, I agreed, and the ceremony was lovely and we were welcomed like long-lost friends. I felt very comfortable and a week later I went back to a service on my own. I experienced a power that literally knocked me out. I thought I'd fainted. They told me I'd been filled with the Holy Spirit and that the experience was called 'being slain in the spirit.' It happened many times over the next seventeen years. It was deeply healing every time. I committed my life to Christ and chose to be baptised. It was in this Christian church community I first experienced a group of supportive, friendly, inclusive women. I could spill my heart to other women and shared the secret of the mess my marriage was in. I'd found a tribe and sense of belonging that had been missing since I'd left work.

When the children were toddlers, I trained as a colour and image consultant after experiencing my own transformation with colour and style in my wardrobe. I excelled at this. I was a natural at talking to women, encouraging them, and helping them feel great about the way they looked.

The shame of being Maori ended abruptly after my brother John had been researching our ancestry for decades. John arranged for Dad and us to meet many of these people. It was deeply moving, particularly for Dad who at seventy-eight finally embraced aunties, uncles, second and third cousins, all much darker than us. The shame dissolved. We learnt more about our heritage, our ancestry, and our land. The land we come from. Our lineage goes back to the Tuhoe tribe known as the Children of the Mist, and Ngati Kahungunu, the tribes we whakapapa to or descend from. There were many healers, diviners, and tohunga (spirit doctors, medicine priests) in my bloodlines. I was forty-three when I finally felt I'd found my roots. I felt like a tree that had a place to grow, with roots that ran deep. I had visions of thousands of strong women who'd come before me and sensed my soul united with them all. It was as if my body and soul had a whole new understanding of the eternal feminine spirit and I felt the blood of those women run in my veins.

I did the Landmark forum that year, a three day personal development course. It's a deep exploration into what it is to be a human being and is designed to bring about permanent positive shifts in your quality of life. I'd been going to counselling, and moaning to the rest of the world about my marriage, but not doing anything about it. After the course I had some meaningful conscious conversations with my husband and realized he wasn't prepared to make any changes or go to counselling with me.

Twenty-three years married to a deeply wounded man was as much as I could stand, and in 1999 I chose to leave him. It took a huge amount of courage to leave, and at times it took even more courage to stay left. It would have fixed everyone else's world if I'd gone back, but not mine. The unconditional love proclaimed at church turned out to be very conditional. One woman said 'Oh, this is just the devil. You must go back to him.' I didn't. I began to explore what was really true for me and chose not to return to church. It was interesting who was there for me at this time.

I was financially destitute. My children, then thirteen and fifteen, chose to stay with their dad so I didn't qualify for government support. I got a job as a disability information consultant with a social services organisation. I began to grow a sense of the Universe having my back, of something bigger than me leading me in the right direction. Our office space was shared with several community organisations, all managed and peopled by women with Amazonian strengths. They had a strong sense of who they were, advocated for the down-trodden and disadvantaged, spoke out at injustice, and helped write policies that made the world a better place. They'd kill to protect their cubs and have a good laugh after the battle. It was the perfect space for me to heal, learn new skills, connect with a different community, and stand tall. They taught me how to drop my fear of being strong, that it was possible to have a voice, be staunch, have boundaries and not be put down for it.

I met a clairvoyant medium running spiritual development classes. I'd always considered anything spiritual outside the church to be evil or dangerous. It took some bravery on my part but I wanted to learn more about using colour intuitively and about crystal healing, so I began attending her classes. It was in one of these classes I first heard the terms Sacred Feminine and Sacred Masculine. We spent time in meditation, connecting with our sacred feminine, and sacral chakra. I learned to connect with the earth and to see her as 'the mother' and myself as an aspect of her. I came to know that regardless of gender, we all carry aspects of the Divine Feminine and Divine Masculine within us. Masculine aspects lead to public power, security, territory, social identity, and the capacity to meet one's needs, while the feminine aspects lead to unconditional love, creativity, nurturing, and emotional and spiritual connection with self, body, others, children, community and nature. When these are out of balance or shut down, we forget to take responsibility for our actions, get lazy with life, or push to make things happen with little regard for others. I now call this the *Unsacred Feminine* and *Unsacred Masculine* but have seen it called the *hyper* and *Undivine* of each too.

I've trained in many energy healing modalities. My intuition and ability to read people and their bodies is powerful. Without fail, every time I do the work of helping others, I'm compelled to do my own inner work. In 2012, I was fifty-seven. As part of a Visionary Intuitive training, we delved deep into our childhood wounding. I observed the beliefs I'd carried forward from my childhood experiences. The main ones were *I'm ugly* and *No one wants to hear what I have to say.* There's always a story behind these beliefs, why they're there and why they're so strong. They were still influencing my life, sabotaging decisions, relationships and my business. The pain of recognising these lies was excruciating. I cried for days, screamed into the ethers at my parents, siblings, schoolmates, friends, enemies, partners, God, life. I got so bloody angry, I finally felt it all and was emotionally wrung out by the end of it. I learned processes where these beliefs, once recognized or brought in to the light, could be collapsed or deleted at their point of creation. This is deep healing energy work. After deeper exploration I chose to install a new truth about myself. I chose *I Am*. I love how unlimited this feels. I saw the truth of me and experienced the rise of the Feminine Divine within for the first time: it was physical at times – a sensation of a power surge moving upward through me, and an awareness of being a part of the collective feminine. I felt new, unencumbered, and free.

The same year I attended a three day Goddess on Purpose gathering. More diving into wounds and seeing how they stopped me from living a life on purpose. We celebrated all aspects of the Goddess – life, birth, death, vulnerability, courage, strength, softness, power, rage, authenticity. We meditated, danced, sang and shouted. I came to see myself reflected in all other women. All women who have been, will be and are now. And I see them all in me. I experienced my own limitlessness.

The feminine divine has a dark side, a shadow aspect, a bit like the yang to the yin. The word 'dark' had scared me away from my fullness. I'd been programmed to believe light is pure and dark is evil. Being a 'good girl' had been an integral part of my existence. It had stopped me leaving an abused, abusive, alcoholic husband because I didn't want to be 'the naughty' girl. Good girls held the family together for the children. In the end I left for the children. I realized I was living a lie for them. The sorting of life in to good and bad categories had flavoured my desire for acceptance. Because creativity and self-expression had been suppressed through my childhood and marriage, I'd developed a secret side of me – stuff I didn't want the world to know about me: dirty secrets, sinister thoughts and incongruous friendships. Untangling shame and guilt have been a necessary practice to heal my shadow self. My reconciled shadow is now an expert secret-keeper, trustworthy, recognising untruths in others easily and noticing when my thoughts are out of alignment with my own truth.

The following year, I attended a Cosmic Womb retreat. I'd become aware of my womb space as the core of me. Twenty of us spent the day in ceremony, honouring the womb space, energetically feeling in to the shame, guilt, and pain stored there. We cleared the bloodlines of these wounds, doing this work for our children and grandchildren and future generations. It was the first time I'd perceived myself as holy or sacred, and I wept at the beauty of it all. I felt as if I'd been to the centre of the Earth and the Universe and I saw myself as an aspect of it all. It awoke in me a remembering of the female ancestral lineage that stands with me today. I took on the healing mantle of several of the medicine women in my lineage that day. At times they speak through me and I often call on their wisdom when I'm working with others or making decisions.

I was inspired to honour my body with deeper integrity. I cleared our home of chemical cleaners, began using only natural hair and body products, chose to eat mostly organic, and stopped colouring my hair. As the colour grew out, I moved through processes of vulnerability, feeling exposed and untidy. Embracing untidy was foreign and a bit exciting for me. It all felt a bit rebellious and thrilling. I wanted to create something to celebrate me. Something beautiful to honour my years, my wisdom, my journey, my body, my soul and my spirit. A close friend, a medicine woman, devised a croning ceremony with close friends who all contributed unique ideas to honour who I am for them. It remains one of the finest experiences of my life.

In 2014, my daughter birthed a daughter and I stepped onto the hallowed ground of grandparenting. I'd tuned in to this soul about four months into the pregnancy and felt a strong soul bond with her. I knew that this soul had mothered me in another lifetime. I felt she was coming back to teach me what she had run out of time to complete in our previous life together. She was waiting to share my breath. I was so excited to meet this wee soul and to *hongi*. *Hongi* is the Maori word for the meeting of nose and forehead, the sharing of breath, the acknowledgment that we are all one. Watching my baby birth a baby was an exquisite experience, watching her take her first gasp looking right at me. I held her, our noses and foreheads met, sharing breath, oneness. Her greatest gift in that moment was when I looked into her eyes. I believed that we move through life accessing different aspects of the Divine Feminine at different stages. What I saw in my mokopuna's[7] eyes were all the aspects of the Divine Feminine already present in her – child, youth, mother, crone – and I realised that that's true for all of us. We don't age into those stages; they're all present in the now. Fully integrated and accessible. Maiden, Mother, Crone.

It's been helpful to read about the many archetypes of the Divine Feminine and to see how each of them show up in me. The warrior, mother, grandmother, sister, secret-holder,

---

[7] grandchild

creatrix, dreamer, sensitive, lover, healer, alchemist, priestess, crone, darkness.

My journey has offered powerful experiences that have equipped me to support others as they explore and heal themselves. My life now is about making conscious choices and I love nothing more than to have conscious conversations with others willing to meet me at that level, without needing anyone else's approval. As an aware woman I feel a responsibility to hold a loving and safe space for others, to collapse their unconscious beliefs and move forward with a new belief in themselves.

Dianne lives on Queensland's Sunshine Coast with her husband. She is an Usui Reiki Master and energy healer with the ancient wisdom of her Maori culture in her DNA. Her spare time is devoted to her mokopuna and walking Australia's beaches.

Janie Walker

Persevering towards the Light

When I was five
I was almost eaten alive,
by a boy with ginger hair
who was standing on the stair.
The other one waited
He sounded elated
As I was passed down
To the funny clown.
His attention was below
And I didn't know.

Discovering my traumas when I was forty years old didn't help. I was being told to look at my character defects, trust in God, and clean house. By another alcoholic mentoring me through a 12-step programme.

How was I to trust in God when God had never helped? God was something I had been told to believe in by my mother, my grandmother, my aunt, and society. Now I was being told there was no other way, that was how you got sober.

The day I told my aunt I'd found God in Alcoholics Anonymous, she went berserk, shouting that the only God is the Lord Jesus Christ found through the Brethren. I wrote her a ten-page letter to let her know I wasn't going to allow people to tell me what to believe in any longer. That was the start of me speaking my truth.

One long, lonely night, my own father, who had waited until my mother had lain unconscious (from sleeping pills and the effects of phenobarbitone she had been on since I was born), left me scarred. The deepest scar of all: not being believed.

"Away out and play with your ropes," was all I heard the next day after telling, which I did. Those ropes eventually metaphorically wound their way around my throat, silencing me and tying my hands behind my back, anchoring me to the earth, so that I would never leave my body again. The eight-year-old forgot, burying the thoughts, the words of denial.

I left my hateful school at fifteen. On many occasions in primary school, I'd been hit by a teacher to the beat of "stupid, stupid, stupid." Her jade bracelet hung on the end of her fat arm which flapped to the beat from her wrist on my head. By the age of eight or nine, I had learned not to tell the truth, especially about abuse.

As an adult and sober about three years, one night I saw a little oblong light. I was drifting off to sleep and was drawn to open my eyes. It sat there, still, at the side of the bed, and I lay there staring at it. I saw it a few nights after that, but I never asked who it was or what it wanted or if it had a message for me. It just was. Perhaps it was shining the way forward, perhaps it was a way show-er, as I was to become later on. Most probably it was warning me about the latest man, and I ignored not just that message but many more I was to receive all through that relationship.

About this time, a lady I worked beside introduced me to angels and gave me a little book. I thought she was crackers. How could angels help me? That last relationship was about me craving attention; I believed at the time that if I wasn't needed, I wasn't loved. He was incapable of love but talked a good game, and it lasted ten long years, off and on.

A few years into my sobriety, I met a reiki master who I also thought was nuts but I had a session or two with her and agreed to do the Usui reiki course to master teacher level. I was sitting up in bed one night reading my manual. I'd emptied a wooden wardrobe in the room when suddenly a hanger started banging against the back of the wardrobe in a rhythm, like it was banging to a song. I dived under the duvet and shouted, "You can just fuck right off whoever you are" and so it did. I stayed under the duvet anyway, and determined there and then not to let ghosts or anything else into my consciousness ever.

After that, a woman took me to my first spiritualist meeting where I got a message from the medium on the platform; and after the meeting another medium came and described my father – a hat he wore, the cigarettes he smoked – and gave me another message. I'd just discovered what my father had done and so I wasn't too happy when he tried to contact me. I sat in three different circles and I always got messages. I never believed I was good enough but I was always giving other people messages; I believed I was supposed to be a healer not a medium. And anyway, I didn't want dead people hanging around me after the coat hanger experience.

By the mid-90s I'd realised I would never be able to have another drink, ever. During my 12-step programme, all the secrets had come tumbling out – the resentments, the fear and anger, and all the trauma that had been supressed.

My mother had died, or rather was told to die, and so she had. On her final day, I had gone to the hospital and was surprised to see my brother sitting on the bed, as he rarely visited. He said I should go home and see to my family. I was taken aback and stupidly did what I went home. My husband questioned this and said I should go back and so I returned immediately to the hospital. On opening the door, my brother was still there sitting on the bed and said that he'd told my mother to go – to die – telling her we were all exhausted. I was shocked that he had taken from me my desire to be with her when she passed.

The year I turned forty, I lost my mother, my sister, my grandmother, and my stepfather. Then I got sober. My husband told me he had lost his drinking partner and decided to find several others elsewhere, eventually divorcing me.

Just before this, after another of his drunken, potentially dangerous episodes, I'd taken the kids and run away to the place I'd taken my mother many times after my father died. It was a pub at the most southerly point in Scotland. It had been dark when we arrived but I knew that once I looked out the window at the sea, I would feel better. With a swoosh, I pulled back the curtains and there was a brick wall. It was an amazing metaphor to how my life was going. On the way back, I stopped in to visit my uncle and left the kids with him while I went for a walk on the beach. I walked across the village road and onto the sand and within a few steps I felt a surge of joy and euphoria charging through my body. All I could think about was the metaphor of the footprints in the sand that I'd learned from Alcoholics Anonymous. I walked and walked, and with each step I got lighter and lighter. I felt like I would be lifted up to the sky, the feeling was so powerful. Eventually I had to return, but I didn't want to leave this immense feeling. I headed back to the road and as

I stepped from the beach to the road it went away. I knew it was a spiritual awakening and couldn't believe that, while my mind was in so much turmoil and despair, I would be able to experience this kind of feeling. My recovery continued, as did my husband's drinking.

I went to see a healer about my anxiety and arrived stressed and tearful. After some discussion she asked me to lie on a therapy bed. I went into a deeply relaxed state. A light burst onto my face but I kept my eyes closed. Moments later she asked me to come back to wakening. I asked her why she had shone a light on my face? She smiled – at my naïveté I suppose – and replied, "The light was coming out of you." I didn't really understand that but as I was leaving I felt like there was going to be hundreds of people waiting for me going out and I felt like a queen. I almost starting walking regally towards the entrance, to an empty street of course, but again I had been elevated by the light.

After that, I joined a world-wide spiritual group in Glasgow and went on a visit to India, the origin of the group. I became vegetarian and celibate and believed in Baba as the supreme soul, and even – according to them – stood in front of God who handed me a sweet as he/she looked me in the eye, a woman Brahman acting as a surrogate for God. We floated around in white saris and meditated all the time. I was more interested though in the street people of the village.

I became self-employed, as an artist, and as a facilitator of writing groups for people who wanted to write without it being academic. This suited me well.

The next years were spent bringing up my children, with very little work and very little money. I had ADD and it caused many sleepless nights, and praying to God didn't seem to bring much peace. I continued going to meetings and following the suggestions of Alcoholics Anonymous, but it wasn't enough for me. I persevered with prayer and meditation, and I believe they saved my life and my sanity. Then I found Louise Hay, *The Celestine Prophecies*, and Hay House.

I have different views on God now, and how we came here to this blue pearl. Each day is a diamond that I plant in the earth. I'm not scared to die, but every minute, every hour, is precious in my conscious wakening days.

Sometimes we have to live in difficult times with difficult people, just to survive. And so it is. And as the cycle of addictions live on for a little while longer in my family, so does hope. My desire is that as many people awaken as possible, before it's too late. And for now, for me, I must take myself to that place, so that I can become as light as that day on the beach, as light as an angel.

May all the lightworkers on our blue pearl shine their lights to awaken the world to the truth and to love.

The sea like my tears
lash on the sand; then God walks
with me for a while

Janie lives in Glasgow; she has two adult children and a granddaughter. Her life is filled with therapy, art, writing, meditation, and beach walking, and helping others through EFT, and hypnotherapy.

Megan Newberry

Namaste

As a child I was scared of the dark. I saw things, I felt things, and the grown-ups would say I had 'an overactive imagination.' I was however moved from the newly converted attic bedroom back to my old bedroom with my younger brother around the age of seven. Even now, attic bedrooms are not a comfortable subject for me.

Before I understood the difference between religion and spirituality, I was brought up in the protestant Church of Wales, going to church every Sunday, and when old enough I was a chorister and a server. I was very traditionalist when it came to church services and any change to this met my disapproval. I was also very black and white in my thinking. When I was sixteen, I told my best friend that if she didn't go to church she couldn't go to heaven. Amusingly, she became a minister of her own church. I have since apologised for my naïve, self-righteous sixteen year old's perspective on life, and how she laughed!

My teenage self was generally accepting of what I had been taught, but I remember getting very upset when the parish vicar said that animals don't have souls and couldn't go to heaven. That I could not believe. And as a Christian, although I believed in life after death, and that if you were good to people you would go to Heaven, this also disturbed me. So, you have this one life, then you die, then you go to heaven. But what's next? Heaven, forever. But what's forever and isn't that just boring?

My experiences with the supernatural in my teens were limited to feeling a big smacker of a kiss on my cheek one morning just as I was waking up, with no one there; and one day when I was crying over a boy and I heard the sound of a tissue being pulled out of the tissue box, and sure enough there was a tissue waiting for me. Both of these experiences, I believe, were my grandfather who passed away suddenly when I was seven, but had a reputation for handing out the tissues during a weepy movie.

My first definitive paranormal experience was on a ghost hunt at *Llancaiach Fawr*, a Tudor manor house north of Cardiff, when I was a student radiographer. We were shown around each room by candle light and told stories of the history of the house, the people who had lived there, and the experiences of the staff working there. —In the great hall, as the guide was chatting, I was overcome with a terrible feeling of sadness, and felt that someone was standing very close to me. I wanted to burst into tears with the sorrow. Afterwards, I told one of the staff my experience. "Oh yes", he said. "That has been reported very often in this room. Only the other day a photographer came to take some pictures and he burst into tears and I had to take him out of the room." Bearing in mind I had been a nervous child and had pretty much taken that into adulthood, when I returned to my fellow students asking where the alcohol was, their question was "what's up with her?"

Later, I visited a psychic medium. She told me about my current ending relationship (for the best) but that I had just met a nice man. I was confused. No? She said "when you meet him, he will talk about a death. Nothing to do with you, to do with him." Not long after, I was with a friend who talked about his Father passing away recently. I married him.

In my late twenties, my dear gran passed away. As I heard the news, I had the feeling of a warm ring starting at different directions to join up and envelop me with love. I like to think of both my gran and grandad finally together again and wrapping me in a spiritual hug before they went on their way.

My heart ached. I'd sat on the floor of my grandparents' empty living room and said my goodbyes to this place of wonderful childhood memories. It was almost a meditation, a way of communing with my loved ones who had passed.

Life was busy with a career, marriage, and home, and then after five years of trying to become pregnant, I amazingly had my son when I was thirty-six. Things were challenging through the trimesters of pregnancy, the birth experience that did not go so well and ended in an emergency caesarean, my son being an enormous 10lbs 5oz, and then being poorly with an infection a couple of days after birth. The midwives said "Oh, he's been here before." The experience taught me that earth angels do exist to support and guide you in your darkest hours, and to believe and stay strong even in the darkest of times.

My first serious health issue was a few years after the traumatic birth of my son, when I was diagnosed with ulcerative colitis. I was distraught as my gran had had colitis so severe that she'd had a colostomy bag and various other complications. She came to me in a vivid dream: I was on the sofa watching TV and I felt an arm come around from behind the sofa around my chest in an embrace. I thought I *know* who that is, and I haven't felt this person in such a long time. I turned and saw my Gran. I believe she came to give me comfort and support and to tell me it was okay.

In my forties, I was introduced to ghost hunting. My nickname in the group was Scooby Doo! I had many experiences that I could not explain, while feeling terrified in the process! When I went on a ghost hunt at *Craig Y Nos* Castle, I assumed it would be the same as my experience at *Llancaiach Fawr*, visiting the rooms and being told stories. But this was full-on, calling on spirit to engage with the group. I was terrified! We were in a dark basement with old gramophone music playing; a glass on the table moved on its own, and when I looked at a young lady opposite me, she had an old face! At one point I asked for a torch to be shined on her to see her actual face again. The person in spirit moving the glass was an elderly lady; we asked yes and no questions. In another room, the table jigged around to questions being asked and requests to move the table. I looked underneath it, surely someone (alive) was moving it! But there was nothing there. It was an extremely uncomfortable experience at the time; I wanted to believe that there were no ghosts, just as I was told as a fearful child. It left me with more questions than answers. I persevered with the ghost hunts as a fascinating hobby. We visited many places, with exciting histories, going where you would not normally be allowed to go. I found that dowsing rods were particularly receptive to me, and I would have feelings in a room, or of a person, very occasionally seeing a black outline of spirit. Sometimes personal messages from family would be conveyed from the hosting medium which was always very special.

I attended a full weekend of ghost hunting that also included past life regression and accessing your akashic records. This was a real eye-opener for me as my experience was truly incredible. In the moment I thought I was doing a terrible job, and during the meditations I cried a lot. Others reported seeing technicolour and rainbows and rabbits and butterflies. My vision was in black and white and I saw a big black dragon flying overhead. I was a knight. I sat like a man and talked, well the same as me but without the social niceties, a rough around the edges, male version of me, telling my friends exactly what I thought. Meditating to the akashic records, my name was Ishtar, and I received a gift, a sword. I was told this sword would appear in my day to day life as a sign that what I had seen was real. Later that evening we had a talk from a historian who talked about Christianity, Easter, and Ishtar!

As I was driving home, I saw the sky with the sunlight through the trees exactly the way I had seen it in my meditation. When I was home, my son asked me to read him his story book from school. "Look Mummy, it's a sword." And my husband looked over and said "Yes, it's a knight's sword."

Clearly there was something going on here. Through ghost hunting, I met the person who would allow me to progress further into spirituality. In the first instance I nearly ran away in the opposite direction, as he introduced himself as a psychic medium with the speciality of dealing with the 'dark side of the force.' You can imagine my horror when he informed me that the things we tell our children don't exist, do. I decided that knowing someone that could deal with the things I feared on ghost hunts and in the dark, was someone very good to know. We are very good friends and with his guidance I have further developed my spiritual practise.

He taught me how to meditate, to create 'a safe place with the light always on,' and how to protect myself and my energy. The first time I meditated at home I went to my safe place and opened the door. There in front of me was a hole, a swirling circle with a winter scene inside. I popped in there and then popped back into my safe place and mentally closed the hole down. I casually reported this back to my mentor. He was pretty shocked and told me that this was a portal, that I was a portal jumper (quite rare) and presumably had a portal in my safe room to practise in. Then it was my turn to be shocked. All those episodes of *Stargate* did not go to waste.

My meditations were often extraordinary. For example, I would meditate and see myself in Ancient Egypt. I felt something heavy around my neck and didn't like it (I am not a fan of heavy jewellery in this life). A word came to me in this meditation—*Nebu*. I looked up *Nebu* and it is the Egyptian symbol for gold. It depicts a golden collar with the ends hanging off the sides and seven spines dangling from the middle. Egyptians believed that gold was an indestructible and heavenly metal. I was astounded! I have discovered that the information you need to find, will find you. Further meditations were of spaceships, other worlds, beings, Egypt again, and dragons of course. During the COVID-19 outbreak I found solace in meditating; in my meditations I went about hugging everyone I know. Try it.

By 2017, I was feeling that things weren't right and there had to be more to the life I was leading. In June I injured myself, tearing my calf muscle. Laid up for a few weeks, I really had time to think. I had had kinesiology sessions in the past and had wanted to learn this myself but life had been too busy. I found a course starting in the September and signed up. I completed the foundation course in 2018 followed by the practitioners' course in 2018-19 and finished as a qualified kinesiology practitioner in May 2019. I still continue with my day job and practise kinesiology when I can.

During my course I had a setback with my ulcerative colitis. I was devastated as I hadn't had any symptoms for a long while and thought I was clear. My tutor worked with me and I had a session that explained why I had colitis. Kinesiology looks at you as a whole person – the physical, nutritional, mental, energetic, emotional, and spiritual. Using muscle testing, it finds imbalances in the body and corrects them. Very often, physical disease has an emotional component. Mine was stored anger in my body – in my bowel – a red, angry bowel. I had never been allowed to express anger, never learnt how to express it appropriately, and because of this lack of expression my body said "Hey! You need to let this out!"

Now I know that in order for my large bowel to stay healthy, I have to express the emotion of anger. Appropriately yes, but express I must. And that goes for any and all emotions. We are taught we mustn't express our emotions but it is so important to do so for our health. Even if you are alone in the car and shout out "I am angry about that" or whatever it is you feel. Let… it… out… And have a good cry every now and then, it's so refreshing.

Becoming a Kinesiologist involved a lot of healing and a journey to understanding and loving myself better. This is a work in progress; we are all programmed from a young age with beliefs, not truths.

From the first time I laid my hands on one of my fellow trainees, I felt the energy It was a "Woah! What's that?" moment. It was instant, as if my soul was waiting for me to try. A soul knows so much; if you have been a healer before, it's about unlocking that ancient knowing within you.

My journey continues with exploring numerology, working with Angel cards, dowsing, continuing to work with healing energy, and increasing my sensitivity to energy and to spirit. Me. The scaredy cat. Doing a spiritual development course.

Sometimes I can channel messages from spirit and I am definitely assisted in kinesiology sessions, working with universal energy, with love and gratitude, with manifestation. Oh, the incredible synchronicities! Just look for them. When starting out in kinesiology, I had my doubts and fears. Should I really be doing this? The morning before I saw a client, my mobile phone went dead, even though it had had 85% charge. When I arrived at the clinic, my car mileage said 8.5 miles. I checked out the meaning of angel number 85. One of the comments was, if you are thinking of beginning or expanding a spiritually based practice, the timing is right. Good encouragement. Later, watching an episode of *Greys Anatomy*, one of the surgeons was having a kinesiology session. The character said that his sister Megan made him go! I laughed! When it finished, I saw that the episode was first aired on the 8th of May. The 8th of the 5th. I had another realisation. I'd qualified as a kinesiology practitioner on the 8th of May.

Megan lives in South Wales with her husband and son, where she practises kinesiology and is training in spiritual development, energy healing, and writing. She loves spending time with her family, meditation, pole fitness classes, watching a great movie, reading, and walking her black labrador, Jack.

Bill Kerins

My Spiritual Journey

I believe we are born into this world with one main objective, and that is to develop and expand our spiritual essence. I believe we have been here many times in different guises, and when we leave our present body, we reassess our experiences and decide whether we will come back to another lifetime or not. This decision depends on how well we learned our spiritual lessons – this life is not about how much money we make or how famous or successful we become; it is about spiritual development. It is about learning.

Believing in an afterlife is the only thing that makes sense to me. Success and money cannot be taken with you. The only thing we take away from this world is experience and knowledge.

I also believe that we are the creators of our lives. If we are built in the image and likeness of God, then we must be creators. We have the ability to create whatever we *need* in life. This doesn't mean though that we can create whatever we *want*.

We create everything we need, not what we want.

This makes sense to me, because when I think about the lessons I've learned throughout my life, I realise that I have created the circumstances required for me to learn a lesson. Here are some of the creations I have created. Some of them are good and quite a few of them are not so good, but they were the perfect creations for the time.

Around the age of four or five, I was subjected to about ten years of sexual abuse. It continued without me fully understanding what was actually going on. In Ireland there was no sex education and I had no idea what was happening to me. I never enjoyed it and I never consented to it; I just didn't know. It was painful, upsetting, and embarrassing, and I wasn't allowed talk about it. It was *our little secret*. It was not until I was around fourteen that I realised that it was wrong, abusive, and demeaning. I suppose it had become normal to me, until one day in school, one of my teachers touched on the subject. I was shocked. I immediately stopped it, but it left me with nightmares and phobias for years, well into my adulthood. In fact, I was well over fifty before I cleared all of it.

On reflection, what lesson was there for me? I learned that I needed to be more aware. I needed to learn what it was like to say 'No.' I learned to respect and care for my body. I also developed a great empathy with others who have been abused, whether it was sexual, emotional, verbal, or physical. This was a very useful attribute to have when I became a teacher and therapist. Had I created all of this at the age of four or five? Maybe.

I was born and reared in Dublin, in a working class family. My father died when I was eleven and my life changed drastically. In one day I went from being a child to becoming an adult with responsibilities. I couldn't understand why this had happened to me. I suppose that was the first time I questioned the justice and love of God. On later reflection, the lesson was profound. I needed to grow up fast and begin to care for my mother. Many people blame God or some other entity for their misfortune. I now realise that, at that time, I must have created the circumstances in order for me to grow up fast and miss some of the childhood experiences that were coming my way. My father didn't die in vain at the early age of sixty-four. It helped make me the person I am today.

In 1963, The Beatles burst onto the scene. I loved their music, but what I loved most was that they were ordinary working class guys like me, and they had broken down the barriers to a better life. I adopted the attitude 'if they can better themselves then so can I.'

During my time working as an aircraft engineer in Aer Lingus, I learned to play drums and played part time in a number of local wannabe bands around Dublin.

I spent seventeen years at Aer Lingus working on Jumbo jets, about ten years too long. We had a saying 'is there life after Aer Lingus?' I had a belief that I wouldn't be able to survive outside the security of Aer Lingus, that nothing else existed.

One day, a colleague advised me to get out before it killed me. Until then I didn't really know that I could leave and find something better. It wasn't the work that bothered me or the workmates, it was the system. I had come to realise that I was destined to remain in the same job with the same old day to day routine for the next thirty-two years. And the thought of that was killing me. So I left and went on unemployment benefits for about eighteen months. I loved it. I had never been unemployed before, but I felt like I had been set free. I could play music, do as I liked, and rest my mind until something constructive and positive turned up. I learned to trust in the Universe. I knew I was being looked after and directed. Had I created that scenario? Maybe.

Since then, I have followed this path of knowing that I had spiritual support and managed to attain a reasonable level of success. I played along with some of Ireland's finest musicians. I enjoyed the small amount of fame that followed and I became a better drummer and singer. Ultimately, I found a part of me that would have remained hidden if not for those early experiences. That part was my spirit. It was not a religious revelation, but more like a spiritual realisation. I realised that I was not alone. During my many jobs, gigs, and travelling, I became aware of another unseen presence that guided me to the right conclusions and destinations.

Examples of this spiritual guidance came in the guise of opportunities to join bands that, on the face of it, were great opportunities to become the pop star I dreamed of. But I turned them down, and for a while, I thought I had missed or messed up great chances. Later I realised I was guided away from a danger that would have led me into a darker world.

The values my parents taught me were always close to hand, and some of the situations I found myself in could have destroyed those values, something I would have regretted for the rest of my life.

I married in 1968, became a father for the first time in 1969, and soon after stopped playing music. I really missed the *craic*, as they say in Ireland, at the time there were more important things to occupy my time and mind.

However, the itch to play music stayed with me and in 1975 I was approached to join a group that gigged every weekend. I jumped at the chance.

I felt at the time that it was a need I had rather than a want. I loved being part of something that gave a lot of fun and pleasure to others. I don't think it was about fame and it certainly was not fortune. I discovered a part of myself that I rarely reached by pushing my abilities a bit further than I thought possible, and I think that was the spiritual awakening that had been missing up until that time. Music filled a hole in my life even though by then I had three great kids and a mortgage. Some would say that they should have been enough and they were more than enough, but they couldn't fill the need to play music and be part of the music scene.

Playing in a band every weekend though came at a cost to my marriage. My wife and I drifted apart, or grew up – I'm not sure which is true. We split up in 1977 and I went downhill big time. I became very depressed and seemed to lose my purpose in life. I told myself that it was all part of the process of living, but still couldn't shake off the depression. Not until a fateful night when I was sitting in my car with a friend.

We had been out for a drink and I was leaving her home. We sat outside her house in silence for an hour. I was just about to tell her to go home when I heard a voice speak to me. It wasn't my friend, but it was a woman's voice, one I didn't recognise. She said very clearly *"You are only growing up, Bill."* I nearly jumped out of my skin. It was so clear and powerful. Immediately, I felt a hundred times better. The depression went instantly. I felt overwhelmed. I had never experienced anything like that before, and only a couple of times since. How could I go from deep depression to bliss in seconds?

After seeing my friend safely home, I drove home on a cloud. The depression had completely gone and it never came back. I took time to examine and question what had just happened. I had heard of people having epiphany moments but I'd never thought it could happen to me. In one second, my spiritual awareness was restored. I no longer felt alone. Someone had spoken to me through the darkness of my depression. I hadn't asked for it or expected it.

Many of the songs and artists I've encountered throughout my time as a musician have helped me go within and ask questions of myself and of life in general. In the same way that poetry and art have an impact on some people, certain songs and music have that impact on me. Instrumental music never really interested me – there were no words to contemplate.

James Taylor, Neil Diamond, Gerry Rafferty, and the Eagles, brought words that touched my heart. The energy of bands like Thin Lizzy, Boston, and the Average White Band took me to a different place. Voices like Eva Cassidy, Paul Carrick, Eric Clapton, and Barbra Streisand put a shiver up my spine. When my wife Patricia sings certain songs, I well up with tears. She touches my heart and soul.

I believe that these songwriters and performers are inspired. When you break down the word *inspired,* it is 'in' and 'spirit'. In Spirit.

Many songwriters have said that the words came in a dream or during meditation. The Beatles song *Yesterday* was an example of this. Paul McCartney claims that he woke up in the morning with the song ready to record. He had been composing in his sleep! He says that his late mother inspired him to write *Let it be. Mother Mary comes to me, speaking words of wisdom, let it be.*

When I hear songs like these, I have to ask 'who is it that really writes those songs?' Is it Spirit using its power to influence or reach those who can't or don't access Spirit?

I love different styles of music and have no favourite. Depending on the mood I'm in, I can listen to country, heavy rock, or the oldies like Dean Martin, Nat King Cole, or Elvis.

But what is it in these singers and songs that makes a difference to my mood? I think it has something to do with the vibrations they emit. Every voice and sound has a vibration. Perhaps a combination of these vibrations resonates with my vibration at a particular moment in time. If I take two tuning forks that are tuned to the note C, and strike one of them, the other one will vibrate as well. This is called resonance. Similar to this, if I hear songs that resonate with my vibration, then it is natural that I sing along with that song.

And so if everything is a vibration, there must be things we cannot see with our eyes. Is this where spirit, or God, lives? Just because we cannot see something, doesn't mean that it doesn't exist.

All through my life I have felt an unseen presence around me. I always believed that it was the essence of Hannah, the grandmother of Jesus. Known in western religions as St Anne, she was one of the Enlightened Ones.

In 1989, I went on a holiday to Cyprus with my eldest son, Sean. I had read about a man who lived there who was known as the Magus of Strovolos. I went in search of him and found him. He was a remarkable man with unbelievable wisdom and healing powers. Some of his powers are described in a book called *The Magus of Strovolos*.[8] We spent two afternoons together, which gave me plenty of time to ask questions. I asked him about past lives, both his and mine. I wanted clarity on subjects like manifestation and self-healing. He had access to his previous lives on earth and could remember and recognise people who had been with him in previous lives, some good, some bad.

When I asked him why I should feel strongly connected to Hannah, he explained in detail my relationship to her and it all began to make perfect sense to me. I believe it was Hannah who spoke to me in my car all those years ago, and she has been with me ever since. When asked about Hannah, I can see her as a beautiful, kindly, loving lady. I can see myself kneeling at her feet and resting my head on her lap. This is where I feel completely at peace and safe.

Because of these experiences, I have no fear of what comes after we die. I believe it is as easy as moving from one room to another. Of course I want it to be pain-free, but I am not worried about the afterlife. Why would I be if Hannah is going to be there to welcome me home?

My life has taken many different paths. I went from Ireland, to Oxford in England. I had the opportunity to become a teacher and influence the lives of many young people. From there to the north of Scotland, where I built a house. I called the house and land *Roundwood*. It had a special energy. Everyone who visited us there commented on the feeling of love, peace, and tranquillity that emitted from the house and land. I tell people that *Roundwood* was built from pure love. I feel that this was my spiritual home. While at *Roundwood* I trained as a hypnotherapist and I now have a successful and

---

[8] Kryiacos Markides, 2003

satisfying career, helping many clients reach their true potential.

I have left *Roundwood* now, but have taken the spiritual essence with me. I now know that wherever I go, and whatever new ventures I encounter, spirit and Hannah will be with me to guide and help me make positive decisions.

Bill is a native of Dublin and lives with his wife Patricia in Co. Wexford in Ireland. He has four children, and is a semi-retired therapist and life coach and the author of '8 Kerinsian Keys to Self Empowerment.'

Aileen Sullivan

Infinite Possibilities

I was born in Scotland in 1964, the eldest of three; we lived in a housing estate in east Ayrshire and I have many happy memories of growing up.

My mother and father didn't attend church as my mum grew up being forced to attend weekly service with her family and she didn't want us to be forced into the same; she wanted us to make up our own minds. However, my grandmother attended every Sunday and I would often go with her.

I was a sensitive and emotional child and I felt very misunderstood and sometimes forgotten about because of my quiet nature. I would always have my granny's support though. Granny Hannah talked about her encounters with Spirit in dreams, and other experiences she had. She chatted in a natural way that brought no fear. Later it allowed me to question the gifts I'd had from a young age.

I grew up loving all religions. When I overheard others talking about Catholics or Jews or Protestants, I would wonder why we couldn't all just get along. I didn't feel that I wanted to follow any religion myself though and I would have called myself atheist.

In the late eighties, I found myself questioning my own existence. I'd entered an abusive relationship and I didn't know how to get out. I couldn't express to anyone how I felt or what was going on. I would walk home from work talking to a higher source in my mind, asking for guidance and help. I'd feel a calm reassurance inside me that I would be alright. I left the relationship and returned home with nothing but the clothes on my back.

Soon after, my gran passed over. She had told me she would be going on a good day and not to be frightened, she would still be with me. I felt tremendous peace at gran dying, although I was incredibly sad. I knew she would continue to help and guide me.

I was asked by one of my friends to attend a spiritualist church and I thought it would be a laugh. I didn't understand what was going on when we meditated, and I would always have one eye open. After a while, I started to get messages from Spirit. At first, I didn't understand them, then my gran started coming forward with information I had not even told her. This was of great comfort and I did feel Spirit around me a great deal.

Then in 1992, my mum took a massive heart attack, and after six weeks in a coma she died. During the weeks leading up to her death, I would have my mum's spirit with me at home. I used to read to Mum and sing, as she lay in her bed in a coma. I fell out with my dad over this as he did not believe she could hear or understand. For me though, it was a very deep spiritual connection. Later I read *The Diving Bell and the Butterfly*[9] and it explained everything I had experienced with Mum. The night before Mum died, I left the hospital with my husband, Peter, and he drove me to Culzean Castle near Ayr and we sat looking out at the sea; I felt very at peace. I had booked a spiritualist reading some time before, and as it turned out, by the time the appointment came

---

[9] Jean-Dominique Bauby, 2008

around Mum had passed. At the reading, I was given a message from Mum, to go to her room and at the top of the wardrobe there was something in a brown envelope. Peter and I found it and took it downstairs to open it; it was a beautiful photo of Culzean Castle, with the view where we'd been sitting the night before Mum's passing.

I spent many years sitting in circle developing my mediumship. A circle is a group of people who come together to develop, in this case, mediumship. We would be taken through individual and group exercises by the medium, increasing our communication with spirit and learning to trust our inner guidance and the guides that came forward.

I have had many messages and signs and visits from the angels and spirit guides. During one service, I sat beside my friend Paul, and there were two mediums up on the platform. I'd been thinking about a friend's illness and focusing on sending her love, when I felt a change in energy in and around me. I started seeing bright white lights around the room and then two huge white angels with expansive wings appeared in front of my eyes; they appeared to be coming out from the mediums. I nudged my friend Paul to tell him what I could see; he told me he could not see anything. I knew from this that my friend was getting ready to leave us.

I have trained as a Dru yoga and meditation teacher and I also completed reiki training, becoming a reiki master teacher in both Usui and Karuna. I have also worked with the angels for over thirty years and trained as an Angel healing® teacher. When the opportunity came up to do the Dru yoga teacher training, I felt guided to apply, asking my angels and guides for the means to be able to pay for the 4-

year course. I was accepted and somehow the money was available.

I have always had other women ask me to train them to do what I do; I've felt myself that I could do more for others if I could teach about angels and angel card readings. I completed an angel healing® course in 2013; my teacher helped me to believe in myself and to trust and allow the angels to flow through me. It felt really empowering to be an angel healer. I learned so much more about the Angels, Archangels, and the female Archangels – the Archeia.

My understanding of the angels is that they come to help people transform and help in whichever way they can. By asking the angels for the help or guidance you require, they come to offer peace to those who are grieving and support you through change and transition.

My family had lost contact with our youngest niece since she was a baby, causing us much distress. I called on my angels every day and night. We started to have contact with her again a few years later and she told me that Malachi had chatted to her and would visit her. I asked her what Malachi looked like and she replied 'short blonde hair, same as yours, and he flies from my home to yours throughout the night. This was my conformation,

Usui is a form of Reiki, which itself is a form of healing and spiritual awakening and spiritual life force energy. Once attuned, the reiki energy flows through your hands and through your own vibrational energy, to yourself, your client, or pet, and even to plants, food and water.

I have had a higher force guiding me since the late 1980s. I believe there is a divine plan and a divine order for everything, and that we must ask, receive, and act. Although we may be guided to work with others to assist us on our journey, we have all the answers inside us. You may have no idea why your heart and soul are calling you in a certain direction. However, if you allow and just be in the flow, you sure as hell will find out. I have a daily practise when I wake up each day, and I express my gratitude for being alive, to the angels for taking good care of me and my loved ones, the planet earth and all those who live on it, for the guidance I will receive throughout that day, and for the motivation to keep up the work I do. I have meditation and yoga practice that I do every day, and eat a plant-based diet.

I am energetically aware of the collective consciousness and I send out light and angels every day, first of all for myself, and then Mother Earth and the world. I am aware more than ever of how the world requires us to change. The world is awakening and transformation has begun.

I walk for miles every day and I like to garden and read. I love nature and the animals and insects alike, and I like to connect and chat with other people. I spend time with my seventy-nine year old father every day.

With global lockdown, Peter and I have become more peaceful, more centred, more aligned, more grateful than ever. We are thankful every day for these gifts.

As I embarked on a teaching journey with Dru yoga, I had no idea how life changing it would be. I was working over sixty hours a week with teenagers who were very troubled, some of whom were suicidal. Most of these young people had experienced trauma and abuse from an incredibly young age, which had a huge impact on them growing up in a society that labelled them as troubled. I had a different perspective on this, having had similar feelings myself growing up, and especially in my teenage years where it appeared to be worse. I knew these young people were misunderstood and required an outlet for these feelings that ran so deep. They needed healing, just as I did, and I realised why I had an interest in working with children, especially ones that had suffered trauma, neglect or abuse.

My training has had a huge impact on the work I do with children and teenagers I am so at peace and full of fun the young people pick up on that peaceful fun-loving nature. There is a saying some people can feel your energy without you speaking a word, they feel your vibration as you enter the room. I have the highest and best intentions for all my young people. They feel that even though I have never said it. I would tend to have a relaxed way of dealing with the children by being able to act in a crisis instead of reacting if and when I needed too. I have an awareness and higher understanding of the young people

I feel my training as a holistic therapist has had a huge impact on the way I work with children. I come from a place of a loving open heart, I am at peace with who I am, I see the child in a holistic sense, the whole being. I've worked with a lot of young people with troubled situations, including with histories of violence. I've never had any difficulties with them or felt threatened in any way.

I used to say 'why me' and now I say 'why not me.' I could not understand from a young age why I could never seem to do anything right or why my life was filled with so much trauma and grief. I now know why I came here. I am here to bring change to the world, to wake people up. To be the change I wish to see for young people.

I know I have survived as I have a purpose to my life. I feel truly blessed to have the life I have, and I have so much love and joy inside of me, and I want only to pass on this little bit of magic I have, to share it with the world.

Please do not waste any time. Do what your soul is calling you to, *now*.

Blessings of love from my angels to you.

Aileen lives in Scotland and works in residential childcare. She is an angel intuitive, channel and teacher, and has many interests in pursuit of the spiritual and exploring her native land.

Bridget Mary-Clare

When the Ordinary becomes Extraordinary

Today is interesting as I'm about to facilitate a webinar on presence, meaning to be present as a soul in my physical body. It's said we teach what we need to learn and the syllabus of soul awakening downloads into daily life.

Yesterday my partner and I were sitting down having a coffee in the garden when he said to me "I've been blowing you kisses but you haven't noticed." My reply was, "I'm thinking about being present but was totally lost in thought."

My life has been a constant challenge to be on Earth in my body, and on many occasions I would have left if I could. My earliest memories as a young child were of talking to people and friends in other worlds from my cot, which understandably alarmed my family.

I was born into a medical family and the whole family focus was on caring for others, which meant no one seemed to have much time for their own reflection or care so life could get quite chaotic. This was not the world of putting your own oxygen mask on first, it was help others with theirs first, no matter what. And there was a fair bit of *no matter what.*

My parents were Catholics, and in a beautiful way modelled certain spiritual practices, like the power of prayer which gave me a certain foundation for my own path. However this structured form never answered the questions I asked myself from a very young age. My mother had me at forty-eight, meaning I experienced at least a dozen bereavements by the age of thirteen. At seven, my father died and I felt totally desperate and tried to get into his grave at the funeral. My mother told me we had to grit our teeth and get on with it. Bereavement counselling for children was unheard of at that time.

I was constantly asking if everybody had died and gone to Jesus, where are they, and could I go and be with them? No one could give me an answer. Death looked a very attractive option, because Jesus was there as well as many others I deeply loved.

Now I see that this was a huge stimulus for my own spiritual awakening. If life had no map and no meaning it felt intolerable to me so how was I to find answers? If I couldn't get answers how could I get rid of these depressing feelings and the emptiness? How could I keep myself going on?

If no answer appears, then we may use an anaesthetic, and mine was food – sweet stuff, as fast as possible, to damp the pain. A spiritual teacher later shared with me: "food saved your life at that point".

My teenage years were a retreat into nature with my pony and it's only in writing this that I have realised Bimbo my pony helped me form a safe relationship and enjoy the peace of nature and the earth. I felt calmer but by my early twenties the nagging began again. Who am I? Where am I? Where am I going?

And the biggest question of them all: "Is there a map for living?"

I began a desperate search for pain relief. I had to find answers. I recalled some of my mother's stories. As she had grown older her spirituality grew and became very universal. I saw family members and friends asking my mother – Rene – to say prayers for them. She kept telling me "I won't leave until you're ready" and "you have a certain job to do here" but what wasn't specified. Rene told me she'd had a vision where Christ appeared, knocked three times (she heard this) on the front door, and when she opened it she saw him asking her to help with his work of love. Rene had replied, "You don't want me," but he said "I am calling you" and so she then said yes.

These experiences, and my mother's incredible faith under all conditions, including when she was in enormous physical pain at one point, gave me a great spiritual resource. I started remembering the results of her prayers and began creating my own prayers, which I would describe as telephone calls to the divine. These seemed to work for a time but then the old feelings returned stronger than ever.

One day in my mid-twenties I woke up feeling very depressed. I thought: I'd like to be dead but I'm not going to kill myself. I never told anyone else as this felt very humiliating.

In desperation, I then deeply surrendered, saying "Okay God, if you are there, please show me the way and free me from this emotional pain. I'm not going to harm myself but please do something and show me the way."

The prayer worked, and soon afterwards I was walking along a main street in Brighton when I saw an advert for hypnotherapy and past life clearing. I wasn't sure my Catholic upbringing would fit with past lives but now I was getting fired up. It was time to review my beliefs. The hypnotherapist asked my finger to lift and rise when I reached the time span which needed healing and we went back and back till finally we went behind conception and into past lives. I saw myself in the French Revolution up on the barricades and being executed. Many energies were cleared and I understood that we may be bringing into this life unfinished energy from past lives. The remedy is always love. If an issue won't shift, it's commonly a forgiveness issue.

My depression reduced enormously, but still I needed a map for living to put this all together, to make sense of it all in order to accept life on earth. Again I asked my question "Please God where can I find someone to help me find meaning in life?" I knew once my life had more meaning it would be easier to stay put.

I understand now that it is the intention and prayer that attract the response. In a matter of weeks my ex-husband heard of a meeting with a spiritual master called Peter Goldman who was running a workshop called *The Practical Mystic*. By now I was beginning to recognise how answers appear, and with huge anticipation I went to the talk. I met Peter, who is now a colleague, and I knew he was able to guide me to find my own answers. Peter's talk gave me a map for finding my own answers, and guidelines for understanding the spiritual laws that govern life, all of which are held within the great law of love.

I experienced the initial joy of awakening. I soon realised that as light enters in it also highlights the shadow or less refined aspects of ourselves, and so a deep transformation began. I was naturally very psychic and one lesson I had to learn was that this level of awareness was not necessarily linked to a level of wisdom. My teacher explained that though many people were encouraging me to train as a medium, this could potentially unground and imbalance me further. I needed to get grounded, to be in my body on Earth, to integrate mind, body and spirit, in order to become a practical mystic.

In my twenties I married and had our son. My husband was a very busy GP and I felt very lost as a new parent with a beautiful young baby. The world of work seemed easy compared to this role. I'd had a ghastly forceps delivery and was exhausted. None of my training as a nurse, midwife, or health visitor, negated the emotional stress or despair I felt and kept secret. I found a way through by giving and sharing support with other parents in a group I created and later expanded as a charity. I would always pray for help in simple, sometimes desperate, words. Answers came – not in dramatic declarations, but as a thought from someone else, or within myself, which naturally unfolded my next step.

The charity was called *Family Friends;* the foundation was to help create breakthroughs in the breakdown of family life, self-help, and mutual support.

I never saw at the time that a bigger plan could be unfolding, particularly on the themes of new forms of family life. I was focused on the charity and a vision of *one world, one family*, and turning our home into a family centre. Meanwhile William and I were spending very little time with one another and by mutual agreement decided to divorce. Initially I was very sad but somewhere in me it felt right. *Till death us do part* was not necessarily about physical death but about a change in form. I knew in myself this action felt wise and loving and that William and I could then continue as parents together. Later in regression therapy I remembered that I had abandoned my ex-husband in a past life and that in this life I had a soul commitment to stay and be together unless change came from mutual consent which is what happened.

I gradually adapted to life as a single parent and became very involved with an international spiritual school and community at White Lodge in Kent.

I found I thrived once I shared and lived with people who shared a common interest and purpose. In the past I had handled my emotional struggles by work, just as my parents had done, but now my emotions were nagging me, and on several occasions my body spontaneously started shaking. Life blessed me again as I then met a teacher called Binnie Dansby whose spiritual work was centred around the healing of birth. She explained to me that my body was reliving my birth trauma, and over time, with regular breath work sessions, I realised states of deep bliss, and also recognised that the way we experience birth has a profound influence on how we experience life, including the way we in turn give birth.

A lot of struggle released from my body and I then knew that this old pain had kept me fearful of coming more deeply into the physical world. In my fifties this was the foundation for my work to support midwives and their clients through emotional education and healing at a private birth centre in London. All my experience in healing myself through many therapies and trainings has in turn helped my clients and students. At White Lodge I undertook all the spiritual psychotherapy courses and sound training. My son went to the Steiner school and life flourished. I was gradually expanding my own soul map for living and supporting others on the journey.

I was beginning to need a higher income than I was creating, so I moved into a small flat rather than a house. A beautiful space appeared near Tunbridge Wells in Kent, although in need of renovation.

I have learnt for optimal results to always request spiritual support, and then pray for guidance. I asked and affirmed the highest outcome for myself and all concerned. When the auction date arrived, I was informed there was a hold up with my mortgage. It was time to call in Archangel Michael and his team.

I asked for immediate help and knew to immediately go to my bank. The queue was huge and the cashier very slow in her responses. In desperation I banged on the counter and asked Archangel Michael to shift this energy. The cashier picked up the phone and immediately called the manager. She smiled to me and said to her boss "I have a mad woman here and she needs help now," and the money was quickly released.

Meanwhile I drove to the auction house where my solicitor assured me all I had to do was sign the exchange document on arrival. I was politely welcomed by the auctioneer who seemed to be talking about irrelevant nothings and buying time. Finally, he was called to take a phone call outside. I felt massive energy rush through my body energy and said, "No I don't trust you. Stay put and sign this document right now." The document was signed immediately, the rest of his staff stood up and cheered me, and the man himself shook my hand firmly, saying "well done."

I lived alone quite happily for sixteen years, working as therapist, constantly learning and growing as part of a spiritual community. One day I saw a workshop in London with Diana Cooper on World Angel Day. As part of the day Diana asked us if we wanted to meet a partner. I thought, I'm okay alone but I will give it a go anyway. The meditation closed with a request to the angels that all blocks to meeting our partner be cleared and a meeting with them be arranged.

The next month, I looked in the newspaper and someone caught my eye. I sent a message and got a written reply from a man who felt like a total no-no, but I realised in starting the process I was showing the universe I was opening the door to meeting someone.

Meanwhile behind the scenes, love angels were at work. A dear friend started talking with the man seated next to her on a long flight, and they chatted all the way and became friends. A short period later I saw the man's business card on her desk and I knew I had to meet him. Months later, Charles and I were eventually introduced. I had by then met him in my sleep state and he felt kind, loving, and familiar. I gradually accepted that my angels were far wiser than me and this was divinely arranged. I have lived in Scotland with Charles for twelve years now, and in that time I can see that his groundedness and practical loving nature have enabled me to be more grounded and safe in my body. The hyperactive and overworking, desperately searching me has calmed down.

Two years ago, I had a lot of pain in my knees which slowed down my walking. I wouldn't recommend creating the need for two knee replacements but they literally stopped me in my tracks. My body took over and I had to pay attention more fully to my physical needs, and it was a great relief. No big plans just a simple enjoyable way of life with time to be. Even if people asked me what's next, I could only say I'm waiting for something – I don't know what but when it happens, I'll know.

On the day of my second knee replacement I arrived in the operating theatre and had received spinal analgesia. I was drowsy and I found myself going out of my body and arriving in another realm of being. I was as awake and even more aware of myself than I am now. As I drifted into this realm of exquisite rose light I felt as if every prayer I'd ever prayed had been answered and every lack or emptiness filled. Nowhere to go, nothing to do; pure being in an ocean of infinite love.

I saw thousands of faces yet we were all one being – just one body. I was aware of my human self and also myself as a light being, two parts joined as one. I wondered how to express this level of love. I especially thought how can I tell everyone *I love you*. I recognised the operating theatre staff and hearing the surgeon's hammer banging, I was called back into my physical body and life.

In the weeks of recovery following surgery I had time to be and to let go of old ways of being and experiencing life. It wasn't as easy as a magic wand removing all physical and emotional pain; in fact I had a wound that took a long time to heal, but I was blessed by healing and prayers from friends and family. In my sleep state, I met a teacher who told me to take time to integrate this experience. I was already trying to set up new courses which wasn't working because I wasn't ready.

Awakening is a constant unfolding, and my own wakeup calls have come in many ways, sometimes like a whispering in the ear, like a soft breeze on a summer's day, sometimes like a repetitive nagging appearing till I get the message, and occasionally like an alarm clock when I would rather go back to sleep than let go some past experience or comfort zone.

If I have one main message to myself now it is to remember *be still and know.* And then: *live the love and the oneness* amidst the challenges of a human life. Turbulence is training, and the ability to travel lightly is highly recommended. I am becoming a practical mystic.

Bridget lives in Aberdeenshire in Scotland, working as an independent therapist and trainer/coach. She has a special interest in sound healing, spiritual discovery, and supporting life transitions from pre-conception through life, death and beyond.

Jane Tuffill

The Darker the Sky, the Brighter the Stars

I have always been very intuitive and tuned into people's needs and emotions, and growing up I realised I was different from others around me. I sensed a world outside of what was in front of us, lead in part by being aware of my nan's energy. I was twelve when she died, and I would communicate with her in my dreams. My mum and I used to joke that my deceased grandfather would pop in to see how we were, turning off the washing machines, walking up the hallway stairs, and other odd little things.

I went to a Church of England secondary school, and thankfully the teachers didn't seem to mind all my questions about organised religion and the lack of strong women within the Bible. I quizzed the local Vicar on the role of women in the church and his view on women becoming Vicar; it was something I was considering. Needless to say, we didn't agree.

I continued to have occasional spirit encounters over the years. I lived in a house that had a part time extra guest. I was aware of my then boyfriend's grandads' (both of them) energy in our home whenever he was going through a rough time, and even saw a reflection of him in our kitchen.

I took a traditional route of GCSE, A-Level, and a practical degree (Business Studies) that wouldn't limit my options. I wanted to break into the tough world of marketing and design, and at twenty-five I became an account manager. I always gave a hundred per cent of myself to my job but the job was never done and the to-do list was never-ending. At twenty-seven I thought I was on the right track. I was on my chosen career path and had purchased my first home with my long-term boyfriend. By thirty I was burning out. I was giving so much of myself to my job that everything else in my life was suffering and I couldn't see how to change it.

By my early thirties, I was getting broody. I hadn't wanted children, but when I became pregnant, I was over the moon.

As I have Type 1 diabetes, I had been liaising with the diabetic team and we arranged a dating scan. I thought it would a simple thing and we would have a little celebration meal out that evening. How different it was. I was further along than I realised – seventeen weeks – but there was no heartbeat.

It was called a missed miscarriage. I had a couple of options available to me, one being to 'let nature take its course' and wait to deliver the baby, whenever that might be, or come into the hospital over the weekend to take a course of drugs to force the delivery. I choose the second option. The hospital and the nurses were amazing and I gave birth on Sunday at 5:55pm. They worked with a charity called Simba which supplied them with a little outfit and blanket, and they wrapped her up so carefully for us, as she was so fragile. To us she was perfect. She is our angel Seren. Small enough to fit into the palm of our hands, but with little finger nails, and long legs. I had had so many hopes and dreams for her.

That weekend broke me. Any defence I ever had was smashed to pieces. I had been given a week off work but took a month, and in truth I needed longer. I didn't go back until we had a private funeral for our daughter, Seren. I will never forget the tiny white coffin which contained some precious items from us and her grandparents, so she wasn't alone.

After that, everything changed. I realised there was more to life then working all the hours under the sun. I had always been able to handle difficult clients, but now it was all too much; the smallest thing was overwhelming, plus I was sitting in the middle of a busy office and it was spinning me out. An empath with no defences should not sit in the middle of an office; I was like a sponge, trying not to soak up other people's energies.

Shortly afterwards, I contacted a card reader; I wanted to make sure Seren was okay, and I needed to make sense of it all. I know a lot of people feel this need when someone passes over and I understand the need for that extra reassurance. I had an amazing session that answered a lot of the questions I had and explained what had been happening around me energetically.

I needed to learn healthy coping mechanisms and be consistent around boundaries. I knew I needed to do something drastic, so I enrolled in learning Angelic Reiki. I was so excited to tap into this new energy and what I thought of as 'making up for lost time.' It made an amazing difference. I learnt the basics of energy, how I was an empath, and how that impacted me on a daily basis. Learning to understand and cleanse my own energy is one of the biggest gifts I have ever been given.

Within three months of starting my training, I quit my job. It felt so liberating, so right. Suddenly I could understand all the different feelings and sensations I'd had as a child, and was excited to be able to connect with the world of energy. I took to energy healing like a duck to water, thirsty for more information, and feeling I was at last doing something that fed my soul. It felt like my soul was remembering from previous lifetimes and slowly freeing myself from so much trauma and limiting beliefs. It enabled me to observe my life, rather than being reactive to it; to realise that at any moment we have choices, and that everything we do is a choice – even doing nothing about a situation is a choice. Our free will is an amazing thing, and so is the love from the Universe. Knowing that at any moment I can tap into the unconditional love of the Universe is truly magical.

When I first started rediscovering/remembering, I would look at other people and compare my journey to theirs, but we all have our own path, and we are all at different points on our path. Life isn't a race. It is to be enjoyed. And even the hard parts can be looked at with gratitude, as those are the moments when we are growing the most, and we are far more resilient than we are often led to believe. We are living in Eden. Our planet is amazing; everything we need has been created – from plants that support, heal and nourish us, to the sun.

I experienced three further miscarriages, each within the first trimester. Each time was different, with different energies coming through. During one pregnancy I experienced an amazing divine love. I was overflowing with love and it felt like it would be impossible for the cup to ever empty. The lesson was that this love is always available to us – the only limit is what we allow ourselves to receive.

I started learning more about the Divine Feminine and how the female body works energetically, and Wow! Do our wombs hold power. As a girl growing up with brothers, I was always a strong feminist. I could easily see that my brothers were as trapped as I was, by society and by limited stereotypes. We are all a mix of energies, and whilst it can be triggering for some (myself included when I first started this work) to refer to the two sides as masculine (action) and feminine (nurturing/psychic), the fact is there *are* two elements within us all that can work in harmony if we allow them. Being too much in one will cause an imbalance in our lives. The raising of the Divine Feminine enables the Divine Masculine to rise also, releasing the current paradigm of toxic masculinity. This is what we are currently seeing.

The more work I do, the more I realise how I have missed having sisters, and how important it is for us to heal in this lifetime from the mistrust that society has been seeding since before the witch trials, pitting women against each other in order to survive.

Rituals have become important to me, acknowledging the changing of our bodily cycles, from maiden to crone. Brotherhood is also important, but that isn't my focus, and I believe men are best leading that, but mutual respect is crucial.

It may sound strange, but I am so grateful to my Seren; whilst I have not been able to enjoy her growing up and experiencing all of her 'firsts' together, she is without doubt one of my guardian angels. I love her deeply, and know that she was the doorway back to myself and spirituality.

My advice:

Please know and accept that you are loved beyond measure by the Universe.

We are never alone, as we have a guiding team that wants to help us, but due to free will, we have to ask them to help us.

Everything is a choice.

Everything happens *for* you, not *to* you.

Each day I am learning or remembering something new. The universe continues to bring people to me that I can learn from, allowing me in turn to assist others. Every time I have asked for help, a teacher has appeared, and I am developing the skills to be able to pass this on.

Life is ever-evolving, and we can be the conscious co-creators of our lives. By working on ourselves, and connecting to the universe daily, we are able to shape the world we live in. We have the power within us to do that; we are not victims. We are powerful. Our measure is not how many times we may be knocked off course, but on how we weather the storms, standing in our sovereign power with gratitude and compassion in our hearts, seeing and learning the lessons presented to us, and owning the situation and our reactions to it.

Jane is an intuitive healer and spiritual teacher, based in the beautiful Welsh valleys. She has a passion for the teachings of the divine feminine, and sisterhood. She is a blessed mum to four cats, and is a grateful tree guardian.

Micque Shoemaker

Because Jesus Loves Me

My first memory of God was sitting in a Sunday school class for preschoolers and mushing my tiny hand into wet, pink clay. We were making gifts for Mother's Day and I couldn't wait to give my creation to my Grandma Dottie. Our teacher was telling us how God made Adam and Eve out of the clay of the earth and so we were using clay to create our own 'imprint' back into the ground from which we were made.

Each Sunday I would dress in my Sunday best and go with Grandma to the First Christian Church in Artesia, New Mexico. It was a squat, one story, pinkish-gray building with a giant cross on top. I attended Sunday school while she went to the morning service. I loved singing the songs and hearing the stories. More than anything, I held onto the fact that Jesus loved me. I sang the song over and over, words barely escaping my mouth in a breathy whisper.

Jesus loves me this I know
For the Bible tells me so
Little ones to Him belong
They are weak but He is strong
Yes, Jesus loves me

Yes, Jesus loves me
Yes, Jesus loves me
The Bible tells me so

I spent most of my days at Grandma's house, days watching her spend every moment being a good Christian wife. She obeyed her husband, raised her children, cared for her grandchildren, and thanked God for the food set before us. A routine of preparing meals, cleaning up, laundry, trips to the grocery store and laundromat filled her days. Sunday was the only day I ever saw her do anything for herself, and that was going to church. She was the kindest, most loving woman I knew and I wanted to grow up to be just like her.

When I was four, my world was turned upside down and Grandma would rock me in her lap, crooning her prayers to God. I took her words to heart, believing that my Father in heaven would intervene and save me. When those prayers were left unanswered, I simply believed that one day they would, because Jesus loves me.

My parents divorced when I was eight and the next six years were a whirlwind of my mother moving us from town to town across the country. Mama never went to church or spoke of Jesus or God, unless she was willing him to damn things that she was angry about. There was little stability in our lives and I lay in my bed night after night repeating the prayers my grandma taught me. I sang the one song I remembered from Sunday school and assured myself that all was well because Jesus loved me.

When I was fourteen, my brother and I went to live with our dad and new stepmother. Once again, each Sunday we would go to church and then have lunch at the local *Tick-Tock* restaurant. I sat through the sermons week after week, not really understanding the preacher, but lost myself in the songs during worship. One Sunday, when I was fifteen, a guest preacher was visiting and his sermon compelled me to step into the aisle when he called on those who wished to make Jesus their Lord and Savior. It was the first time I felt a longing and a personal connection to what I'd been taught and I wanted to be saved. My stepmother stopped me as I made my move toward the aisle. She gripped me by the upper arm and said *No!* She hissed in my ear that I would not go up alone. We were a Christian family already and my going up would be an embarrassment. I stepped back, bowed my head, and hoped that God would save me anyway, since walking up to the altar wasn't an option.

For years we continued going to church each Sunday, sitting on hard pews learning more about the bible and how I needed to live like a child of God – a dutiful Christian, faithful to what I was being told each week, but longing for something more.

The summer I turned sixteen we moved to Oregon. We found a church and once again, every Sunday, we sat through a sermon and then went out to eat. The *Tick-Tock* was replaced by *King's Table*. God was a weekly staple in my life for an hour each Sunday. I knew the stories, knew right from wrong, and dared not commit a sin to save myself from eternal damnation.

A few months after moving to Oregon, I met a local group of teenagers who belonged to a bible club at school. I started going and started to learn more about what Christianity was about when not confined within the walls of a church. Several of the kids were siblings and preacher's kids. They invited me to come out to their youth group that met once a week at their house. It was there that I was finally able to fan the flames of that first spiritual awakening when I was fourteen and wanted to answer the call to be saved.

The songs they sang weren't found in a musty book in the back of a pew. They were songs filled with the adoration found in personal relationships. It wasn't about one person telling a group what to believe. There was a lesson each week, but that lesson came with examples of how it related to our daily lives. Instead of being told how to live, it was an experience of sharing, asking questions, and identifying how it all fit into my life. My conversations with two brothers, Rex and Kendall, made me hungry for a close relationship with my God and His son. I believed, but a nagging voice kept asking me why. Did I really believe or was I just accepting what I had been told throughout the years? Did Jesus really love me?

After high school, I was a bit lost. I had no plans and spent the first year working near home and hanging out with friends who had also graduated. We had all attended the same Tuesday night youth group in high school and now continued to meet and worship as the guys played guitar and harmonica and we harmonized our adoration to the heavens. I needed the fellowship with friends, it was where I found a peace and stability in my life that wasn't always there. I still needed to learn more about why I believed though; I needed to make that decision for myself and not just because I was raised to believe.

A year passed and my best friend was planning to attend *Christ for the Nations*, a private theological school in Dallas, Texas. I'd never thought about going to a school of theology, but here was an opportunity to learn more about why I believed, or if I even did. I signed up and we left Oregon for Texas.

Over the next two years I found out even more than I imagined existed. My experience of worship extended into dancing before the Lord, raising my hands and speaking in tongues. In class I learned about other religions and found common threads through many. It made me start to wonder if the spiritual realm was actually something much simpler than what the religions of the world had made it. Once man became involved, did it become a matter of which faction was right and something to war over? When you remove the little details that differentiate one religion from another, are we then left with the one common element of our Creator and the resolve to live a life of goodwill toward one another? For me, it resonated deeply.

I joined a group who travelled and sang at churches across the country, ministering to church groups and testifying what God had done for us. Our leader would often shudder when I felt compelled to speak. Rather than the expected 'standard' for a testimony, I was known to call people out and question the sincerity of their walks in faith. It all stemmed from what I observed. There were those proclaiming to live a life honoring God but the evidence of their actions suggested otherwise. I was beginning to witness the flaws of man hidden in the shadows of the church.

I graduated and the years passed. Each time I moved I found a local church to immerse myself in, and time after time my observations deepened my skepticism. At some point I stopped going because I couldn't see the point anymore. Inevitably, the very people surrounding me in church on Sundays lived a counter life during the week. The hypocrisy was hard for me to accept. My belief in God didn't waiver though; I still believed and I knew Jesus loved me.

God's mercy became very real to me after a motorcycle accident left me with a broken body and months in the hospital. I have no memory of the accident. My last memory before we were hit was a bright light, and then nothing until the ceiling tiles of the trauma hospital were flying by above me. And then nothing again for weeks. I was told by people who were there that I was making unreal, animal-like noises that raised goosebumps on their flesh as I lay trapped beneath the car. I answered the questions from the first responders as they kept me alive, my body twisted and broken, but I remember nothing. I believe that was God's mercy and grace.

Recovery was painful and slow. My life changed forever. The activities I loved were no longer possible for me and friends quietly disappeared when it was apparent that it would be a while before I was on my feet again. It takes a special kind of person to keep coming back when you are not your best self and the associated pain is overriding your senses. You do find out who really loves you in times like these, and in my case it felt like the last man standing was God.

The year after my accident was riddled with changes that left me with no sense of self. My career was behind me and I saw nothing in front of me. My relationship was floundering and I was a shell of my former self. No substance, no stability, and no one around me who could relate to what I was going through. Saying that I was lost doesn't define the void that enveloped me and the sheer loneliness that threatened to swallow me whole. For the first time in my life I wondered if God had indeed forsaken me. Little did I know that very soon, on a flat playa in the middle of a desert, one man would wake me up and shake me to my core with just two words.

Burning Man 2005. The playa lay below, as my car rounded the curve. Thousands of people spread out before me in the afternoon heat, the dust billowing beneath the cars forming a line to get through the entry gates. As I approached, several people were taking tickets and pointing folks in the right direction of their camp. Most were in polo shirts and khaki shorts with bandanas tied over their noses and mouths with dark sunglasses blocking the sun that was beating down.

A slim man in front of me, wearing a long loincloth and a necklace of turquoise beads, danced his way to my car. He smiled widely and bowed deeply. He looked straight into my eyes and I felt goosebumps raise on my arms. His eyes were kind, the kindest I'd seen.

"Welcome home," he murmured. Just two words. Two words that released a tidal wave of emotions I had buried for the last year. I tried to choke them back but could not. The acceptance I felt bowled me over and I wanted more than anything for his words to be real. He never said another word, took my ticket, squeezed my forearm with one hand, and spread out the playa map, circling my camp and the location of the temple.

I found my way back to God in that temple. Sitting cross-legged somewhere near the center, I wrote down all the things I needed to let go of and release to Him. Unburdening myself of the guilt and shame I had been carrying. Releasing my fear and trusting that He would know what to do with it. In those moments, I knew that God had not forsaken me. He was right where I had left Him. I tacked multiple pieces of paper to those temple walls until the temple burned five days later.

I haven't attended a church service in over thirty years and feel closer to God than ever. My reverence and belief aren't based on what I find between the walls of a church building. I'm not opposed to attending a church service; but I worry that my focus will turn to the flaws of men surrounding me.

I hope to find a church again one day as a place to continue to worship and socialize with others, but I have some work to do first. I have projected my own self-criticism and lack of trust in myself onto others, especially those in the churches I attended in my past. As human beings we are flawed and make mistakes, no matter what our faith. I held myself and others to standards that were impossible to meet. If that type of living were even possible, then where would forgiveness come in?

My current walk with God is a daily work in progress. Do I know that Jesus loves me? Yes. That I am confident in. My place is not to judge the actions of others or myself. My place is to live in such a way that I am strong and confident, loving myself, and giving myself a break when I fail. Only then can I be there to support and uplift others.

I feel and see God all around me, especially when I am alone on a beach watching the waves roll in. I can see and feel the enormous power in the water, its depths filled with energy and life that comfort my soul.

While my grandma had her own flaws, she lived a life of noble purpose grounded on her faith in God. She was kind and honest, taking care of others, but not forgetting to take care of herself. She was loved by everyone who met her, which would probably surprise her. Her presence made you want to be a better version of yourself.

Today, I feel like that's what God wants of us. To get to know Him, spend time with Him, and come to a place of self-acceptance and peace, His presence in our lives moving us to become better versions of ourselves. If we all did that, maybe the differences tearing us apart would fall away, leaving us with mutual acceptance and love.

Until then, I will continue to live toward that purpose. Because Jesus loves me.

Micque lives in the Pacific north-west. She is a proud mom who loves her family and finds her strength on the beaches, soaking in the beauty and the sounds created by her Maker.

Wendy Bath

A Sense of Belonging

Why did I feel I just didn't fit? I was a square peg trying to fit into the round hole where I was expected to happily find my place.

From a very young age, I knew I was an empath. I'd never heard the word or known of its implications; I just knew I felt my own emotions deeply. I felt other people's emotions and I was a people pleaser. I didn't understand why I was a victim of bullying and why the world seemed so uncaring and didn't have the capacity to love like I did, or love me the way I needed to be loved.

It wasn't until my world came crashing down, when I was diagnosed with Fibromyalgia, that it all started making sense to me. A dear friend took me to one side, as she'd seen where I was emotionally and physically, and said she could help me. The fact she's called Wendy too has always amused me, but there she was, my guide into the next magical part of my life. Turning fifty seemed to be a catalyst too. I had to stop living my life at a million miles an hour, taking on other people's worries and energies whilst depleting mine.

I was adopted at the age of seven weeks. My adoptive parents have been wonderful and have given me the best opportunities anyone could dream of. They are my parents.

They did the best job they could at raising me, but some of the choices they made on my behalf didn't feel right for me. I felt a deep need to conform, to be their 'good girl.' I had to as they'd taken me into their family when my birth mother had 'abandoned' me. I never questioned anything; I did as I was told. I didn't feel worthy of love, as the one person who should have loved me had left me. I know now that all of that is rubbish and I'm free of it, but as a child and young adult, I felt this deeply and carried this weight of having to prove myself to be loved all through my life, until Wendy started to unpick it all... those self-sabotaging thoughts, all the pain of not being enough, of not fitting in.

Now I'm proud of not fitting in. I'm comfortable in my own skin and relish the wonderful powers and gifts I never knew I had. Being brought up in a Scottish Presbyterian family had well and truly pushed those gifts away.

The most amazing part of my path to discovering the real me, came when I made the decision to look for my birth mother before I turned fifty. It had niggled away, that annoying missing piece to a nearly complete jigsaw puzzle. I'd never searched before because I didn't want to hurt my wonderful parents. I knew it would cut my dad to the quick. So I had to do it in secret. It was something I had to do for my own peace of mind, my own identity, and the heritage of my genes. There were so many unexplained things in my life that had to come from my birth parents.

So, on my forty-ninth birthday, a dear friend, who held my hand through the whole process, drove me through to Registry House in Edinburgh where I had an appointment to open up my adoption papers. I was quite numb, not really knowing what to expect. My friend was more emotional! When I held my birth certificate in my hand and saw the name my mother had given me, I felt a wave of relief. Something huge lifted off my shoulders and I finally belonged. I didn't cry, I touched my mother's signature (we'll call her Andrea) and knew that the connection broken so many years before was mended. I felt calm and peaceful, knowing I'd needed this.

We did more research into my birth family using the birth, marriage, and death registers and found a big family out there, one not far from where I was sitting. Finding my birth father was going to be a bit more tricky as it involved English registers even though my father – we'll call him James – was a Glaswegian, like my mother. Facebook was a huge help and through tracing one cousin with an interesting name, I finally found my mother. A beautiful picture of her looking out at me. I sent her love through the ether.

Surprisingly, the connection that mattered was going to be with my father, so it didn't hurt when my mother decided not to contact me. All the hurt of her abandoning me had gone, I knew she was young, from a difficult background and the most loving thing she could have done was give me to a family who could give me a better life. I thank her in my prayers for that choice.

We found my father through an old newspaper clipping. He had married my mother and they'd gone on to have more family. I was excited to see that his musical talents were incredible and of note back in the 70s. My, and my children's, musical talents came from him. Unfortunately, he'd died young and I was sad that I wouldn't have the chance to meet him.

Wendy, after a session of EFT (Emotion Freedom Technique), which had worked wonders for my healing by working through all the unnecessary baggage I'd been carrying through my whole life, gingerly asked me if I'd ever had cards pulled for me. I'd always shied away from tarot or the like as my Presbyterian background had put paid to any dabbling in the 'evils' of these pagan rituals. I rebelled and decided I was now free to make these choices for myself. I agreed and so she started shuffling her deck of Oracle Cards. I don't remember the exact cards, but remember how they made me feel. They totally underlined the lessons I was learning at that time. Suddenly my interest was set alight and I enrolled in course to learn to read them myself, something I have pursued over the years since and I'm now a certified angel guide.

All the energy work that I'd done played its part in opening up my gifts, in turn opening up a whole new world for me. I met with my social worker, who gave me more information about my birth and adoption from the forms my mother, Andrea, had filled in. She had put down a different man for my father, one who maybe would have sat better in her parents' minds as he was a Protestant, unlike the man who was in fact my real father, who was Catholic. In the past, Glasgow was, and still is to a lesser extent, a hotbed for sectarianism, and the thought that their young daughter had slept with a Catholic would be unthinkable. It was very firmly stated on my adoption form that I was to be raised a Protestant. I told my social worker about the information I'd found and why I thought her records had the wrong father. There was something intuitively telling me I was right about my birth father. She agreed to contact Andrea, and was so supportive when no acknowledgement came back. I'm fine about Andrea's choice. She has her own life and I'm no part of it.

On the way home, Wendy asked, a little less gingerly, if I'd ever seen a medium. Again, my ego burst in, shouting at me not to go there, but the rebel who listened to my intuitive voice, allowed that idea to enter my thoughts. I sat with it for a few days and made an appointment to meet an extraordinary lady who made the connection for me. I was destined to meet James! Eleanor told me some amazing, private things about my life. My adoptive, paternal grandfather came through and she described the sound of the tackety boots he wore to work. He had so much to say about the choices that had been made for me as a child and now he realised what his part had been in that. I was speechless. Family karmic cycles at work.

The connection that changed my life came when Eleanor asked if I had a father who had passed and one still alive. My heart started thumping. I was shaking and my skin felt like it was lit up and shimmering. James had come to talk to me. He said I'd always been his daughter even though he didn't know of my existence. I felt so loved in that moment, something I've never let go of. It was the unconditional love I'd never felt before and I knew I was with my father. He told me about all sorts of personal things and that he always saw me at the cartwheels. It wasn't until years later I noticed two cartwheels on a house up the road from me.

The biggest confirmation came when he said he'd send me a bumble bee! How on Earth was he to do that! It did make me smile, but he knew my love for nature, and funnily enough, my dad has a connection with the bumble bee too. A nice synchronicity.

Three days later, on a cool, early spring day, when very few insects had woken from their winter slumbers, I got out of my car and a huge bumble bee flew towards me. I had enough time to watch its progress towards me and to realise that this was from James. I didn't flinch as it flew very closely around my head about three times before slowly buzzing away. I said aloud, "Hello, James!" It felt so natural and so beautiful. A really strong affirmation that he was with me and going nowhere.

I've had an amazing relationship with James ever since. As I opened up more energetically, and looked into how it all worked, (learning to love myself and listen to my soul voice, connecting with my Angels and the Divine), the gifts I was given for this lifetime became stronger. I trusted the messages I received from my cards, often knowing which cards would appear before they emerged. My claircognisance, clairaudience, and especially my clairsentience, grew. I started to feel the energies of the Angels and those in Spirit. I asked James to let me feel his energy, and it was like a small spider crawling through the hair on the right side of my head. I wasn't sure at first but as our connection and my trust grew, I started to feel it more strongly. He was a huge support to me as I battled difficult days of fibro flare-ups and life challenges, but I also came to realise that he was respectful of my space and when the Divine was guiding me to make my own choices, he left me to it. I started to hear his voice in my head always cheering me on and giving me the unconditionally loving support I needed. What a beautiful connection we have.

I don't fear death now. I know there's so much divine love awaiting us all. All will be well when we return to the stars with our guardian angel. In my angel guide course, I learned that we are made from stars. We once danced in the stars with our guardian angel who wrote our soul contracts with us before our birth. I find that comforting, and I know I also have James's energy with me too.

Sadly, I lost my dad in May 2020. I miss him. His physical presence at the kitchen table at his beloved farm is no longer there, but sometimes in my mind's eye I see him working away at all his papers. My relationship with him had been strained at times, especially when I stretched my wings and questioned him about his outdated views and his need to control everything. He knew I was often right, and at times praised me for my wisdom and guidance for our family. The day he said "I love you too" will stay with me forever. The day I received a phone call in the wee, small hours to say he'd died came as a huge shock and I was devastated to lose my dad. I wondered if I'd be able to have an energetic connection with him as I did with James.

I didn't have very long to wait. And it was so beautiful. I had popped over to the farm to make sure my mum was okay. She told me a hare had hopped past the patio doors that morning. I said, "That'll be dad, saying hello" and mum agreed.

I have an energetic connection to my dad. The spiders in my hair are much stronger. I asked if James and my dad are together and the answer was a resounding "Yes". All is well.

Wendy lives in Perth, Scotland, where she has been a primary teacher, and now works with women to help them find their voice. She sings and plays music, and performs with her local amateur theatre.

Shelly O'Connell

The Truth Meant Finding Me

In a moment of honesty and awareness, I said to my husband, "I kept you but I lost me." A few days before I spoke those words, I received a photograph. It was of me, taken many years ago when I was the student government president in college. Mine was not the traditional path to college as I didn't begin college until I was in my early thirties. At the time I was already married with two children.

When I looked at this photo, what struck me was my light. I was a radiant, shining light. I could see it so clearly when I looked at the picture but I didn't even know it back then. 'What happened to you? Where did you go?' These were some of my immediate thoughts as I took in this younger version of myself. But of course, on a deeper level I knew. I absolutely knew where she'd gone. She was in hiding and it was me who put her there.

I initially placed her there for safekeeping while I licked my wounds and raged against the betrayals and injustices meted out to me. Ripped open, bleeding and raw, I spent two months flat on my back in bed because I had sprained my lumbar muscle. The slightest wrong movement sent spasms of pain throughout my body. While that was taking place on the physical level, behind the scenes my emotional and spiritual health were taking a beating. I was sobbing, angry, and hurt to my core. I felt abandoned both by people I thought were true friends and by Spirit who seemed uncharacteristically silent.

It took those months and some additional time for me to realize that I was waking up in a deeper way. Now I was beginning to see that I allowed people to use me, to take advantage of me, to hurt me because I was not honoring myself. Many times I saw exactly what was taking place and addressed it but chose to believe their lies; other times I shined it on, meaning I let it slide even though it was wrong. In order to make this work, I had to pretend that the relationship was other than it really was. I stood down on my light thinking it would make it easier to be in relationship with them and sometimes that was true. But it cost me being in relationship with myself. I was no longer able to pay that price.

I understood that in order for me to move forward I had to spend some time looking back. The photo was the doorway to traveling back in time to my hidden light of self. I let all of those feelings wash over me and then I began to remember. During that time, I walked the halls and grounds of campus surrounded by tall beings of light that I call angels. They were not visible but their presence was incredibly strong. I felt supported, inspired, and deeply loved by them. It was beautiful.

Most of the students and faculty responded to me with curiosity and welcome. I was given the most amazing opportunities and felt grateful. Information and guidance came through from the angels and I often shared it with people. Because of being in the position of student government president I became highly visible. The college put my picture everywhere and local newspapers ran it too. The result was many people who I did not know recognized me and would approach me all the time. They always had some idea or concern that they were hoping I could address. It was interesting because with the help of the angels they were undertaken.

The connection and awareness of the angels came after I started college the year before. It began by someone calling my name. I would hear, "Shelly" and look around for who it was. There was never anyone there even though it sounded as if they were next to me. At first I shrugged it off thinking I was imagining things, yet it kept happening. I came to understand that it was the angels calling to me. I wasn't crazy; instead I was at the beginning of a spiritual journey.

I began meditating as a way to open to the angels and to myself. During one meditation, I was guided to go outside. I found myself in a natural circle of trees at the back of our property. A woman with long white hair spoke to me in the meditation. She showed me a small hut that I was to build and told me that women would come here to dream and heal.

Not fully understanding, I shared the meditation with a friend who said it sounded like a sweat lodge. I had no knowledge what that was so they showed me a picture. It was exactly like the hut in the meditation. My friend explained that it was a Native American sweat lodge where ceremonies happen for people to pray. We did build that hut or lodge as I now knew it was called. It was a dream lodge not a sweat lodge and women did come there to dream and heal.

A few months later, I had the opportunity to attend a sweat lodge.

An Abenaki Native American elder was hosting a traditional women's teaching that weekend. It was as if everything I had done in my life, the advocacy for women and children, my personal beliefs, all that I had experienced to that point in my life, culminated to a single point. I was aware that my life had changed. The weekend and those teachings were powerful, beautiful, and transformative for me.

When I went home, I tried to tell my husband about it but the words could not convey the depth of what occurred. In frustration I said to him, "No. You don't get it. My whole life just changed." And the truth was that it had.

Prior to traveling to that place, I knew next to nothing about Native American people, their beliefs, practices, or ceremonies. The next thirteen years taught me much as I journeyed there over and over again. I met people from all over the world, elders who led many kinds of prayer ceremonies that took place there, and a diverse variety of people who came to participate and to pray.

Very early in my travels to that beautiful land, I became aware of the tremendous amount of work being done to prepare for, participate in, and clean up from what were often large gatherings. The majority of this work was being done by the woman elder who owned the land where these ceremonies were held. Her grown daughter helped too. After asking her if she needed help, it became my practice to arrive early to assist her with all of the work.

It was during those times that I began to learn about the ceremonies. Through the years, as we cut material for prayer ties, cleaned the house, built new sweat lodges as needed, and took care of the elders and numerous other things that occur in order to make the ceremonies happen, I was taught the intricacies of the ceremonies. Every elder I met always welcomed me, and they shared their wisdom, time, and laughter too.

I was told the ancient stories of how the prayer ceremonies came to be. Many of the ceremonies were given when things were happening that caused people to be out of balance. So the ceremonies were and are a way for people to be in balance, or as I was told, to live in 'right relationship' with all of creation. 'Right relationship' means living in harmony with everything. To do so, the people had to remember the original instructions for living.

Once, as we were prepared for a ceremony inside a tipi, I went to see the elder running the prayer ceremony. I asked the elder if he needed anything. He told me to sit down, so I did. There were people all around outside and in the house getting ready for the ceremony that would soon take place, but at that moment it was just him and I inside the tipi. He was laying out some of his sacred tools. This is the story that he told me.

Today we have all of these ceremonies. It wasn't always this way. My people, the old ones, tell a story of how it was, back in beginning. They say it this way: "Creator gave us life, gave us everything, everything we need to live. What can we do?" They wanted to express their gratitude, do something to honor what Creator had done for them. So they looked around. Everywhere they looked they saw beauty. That too was a gift from the Creator. The people again thought of the gift of life, everything that they needed to live and all the beauty given from the Creator and all they could think to say was, "Thank you." If we only remembered to say "Thank you," we would never need to have another ceremony.

We sat there looking at each other and I was conscious of how simple and profound his teaching was. I still consider it one of the most powerful teachings I ever received. I thought about how complex we make it. Both the ceremonies and life are intricate.

He had traveled quite a distance from the south-west to run this ceremony. People came from all over to attend. The prayer ceremony would begin at dusk and go until dawn, and then there would be a feast. Everything would be taken down and put away. People would go back home. The house would be cleaned. An incredible amount of effort. I knew we were only halfway done with the work because the ceremony had yet to begin.

Essentially he was telling me that I was working too hard, making it more difficult than need be. Could it really be that easy, I thought? Then I realized that his sharing let me know that I could make it that way. With that comprehension I smiled at him and said, "Thank you." He nodded in acknowledgement and I resumed my duties as medicine helper.

I didn't seek out being a medicine helper, or apprentice to the elder. I had no idea what that term meant when I started showing up to help the elder. I simply came, did what was instructed, asked questions, and tried to take it all in.

For quite a while I was oblivious that I was in that role. One thing that I noted was all of the elders who came to stay and run ceremonies treated me differently than the other people who came to be a part of the ceremony. They were always patient and kind with everyone and would answer questions if someone asked them. With me they took time to share and explain a teaching, or story that contained a teaching. They would invite me to sit down with them as if I had all the time in the world and nothing else going on. In reality the opposite was true. I wonder now if that was their way of giving me some rest?

Often I would think, "Why are they treating me differently?" One day it dawned on me. With comprehension, I said out loud, "Oh!" From that point on, the elder I assisted began directing people to me with their questions. "Ask Shelly," was her standard response.

I am grateful for all of those teachings, gifts and beauty-filled people I encountered during that time.

When I embarked on this spiritual journey, it was like walking on a cloud. Everything was sweet and buoyant. It felt like rays of golden light shining on me and from me. Angels called my name. They supported and guided me through my days. No one told me the bit about being broken down, or the 'shedding' as I like to call it. I was unprepared for it. In retrospect, I think it is this way because there is no way to get ready. I had to live it and feel my way through it. It was raw and messy and quite painful. Made so mostly because I had to face the truth about my relationships which meant I had to release and grieve the stories I made up about them.

I believed one hundred percent that my husband was madly in love with me and had my back. In truth, he was a man who came on to other women in my presence and lied to my face. He took a spiritual practice and made it a competition that he played against me. In my version, the elder I thought was my mentor and friend, in reality started all kinds of reactive behavior once people did begin asking Shelly, as she had instructed. The friend who in my story was a kindred spirit and loved me as I loved them, in actuality was jealous that I was the medicine helper and apprentice that they thought was their rightful role.

It can be hard to face the truth. When I did there were some difficult choices to be made. I removed my support from that elder and left the community. The friend is no longer in my life. In both instances I attempted to express my feelings, and create an opening to hear theirs, in an attempt to move forward in healthy ways, but it was not to be.

My husband and I did find a healthy way forward after he had his own personal awakening. Through his sharing of it and my own reflections, I have come to see that each person has their own wounds, growth, shedding, and healing, to undergo in their own timeframe. Their place on the journey doesn't have to limit or diminish my own. That only happens if I allow it. In all of these relationships I participated in not honoring myself until I could see more truth.

Then the storm came to me in the form of loud sobs and tears of release. It provided the rain to wash away the sludge of my false self. I have reclaimed the radiant bright light of myself. She is burnished with wisdom now and gleams with dazzling light. That alone makes me grateful for it all.

Shelly is a life coach, engaging women with their own wisdom to accomplish their goals and dreams. She lives in Northern California where she enjoys being in nature, painting, drawing, and expanding in ever increasing beauty.

Alwyn Tilston

Out of the Darkness ~ Into the Light

I've had many spiritual experiences since I was a small child, but didn't understand them or have anyone to talk to about them. My first memory is of seeing a moving fairground on my bedroom wall. When I was about five, I had a thought that I didn't belong in the family I lived with. I had a constant dream of trying to run away but getting slower and slower and getting nowhere. I didn't talk about these thoughts to anyone.

When I was thirteen, my mum had to go into hospital. The day she was to go, I couldn't look at her because I knew she wasn't going to come back. When my dad came home from the hospital, I was sat on the settee and I watched my whole being come out of my body, leave the room out the front door, and run down the road. For ever after I was looking for my mum and waited her to come around the next corner. I often felt someone was behind me. There was a lot going on for me at this time, including years of abuse that had already occurred and would continue for several more years. I never shared this with anyone.

I married at nineteen, I thought for love. By the time my third child was born, I was in a very unhappy marriage and clinically depressed. After nearly twenty years of marriage, I knew I wanted something more. Within a year, I had divorced and found a lovely new partner and a new life.

The following year, I began going to a spiritualist church for meditation and to learn about mediumship.

A year later, I was in so much pain from head to toe that I was unable to stand or walk properly or sit down. Nothing I did would shift the pain.

Ultimately I worked with Bowen therapy, and as I understood from the therapist, it was a treatment to relax the muscles. It was gentle and non-invasive, using the fingers and thumbs in a rolling movement at various parts of the body, as well as bringing hands and feet together to see if the body is in alignment. I had five sessions and felt 'opened' up. Like I had been waiting for this to happen.

This really was the beginning for me. After our Bowen sessions, my therapist, Kate, suggested kinesiology. I would go into a meditative state, feelings would come up, and sometimes I would cry and not know why. Sometimes I had past life experiences and my body would often 'crash,' meaning it was all to much for me at that time. During this time, I also changed my diet, eliminating sugar and becoming vegetarian for a while, which helped with my wellbeing.

I was introduced to the colour system of Aura-Soma, plant and crystal energies in water and oil-based liquid, with two separate colours that mixed together into another colour when shaken. This system was developed by Vicki Wall in 1983 at the age of seventy. Aura-Soma is a tool to help us to understand ourselves at a deeper level. It's a non-intrusive, self-selective system in which colour is the key.

I tested for the combination of Magenta/Royal Blue Spiritual Rescue. This bottle is about bringing clarity into feeling about your life. It brings deep peace when your resources have been depleted. Applied to my right temple it certainly bought me peace and I went into complete relaxation.

Another was B1 Magenta/Blue Physical Rescue. This is about peaceful communication with that which lies within us, bringing a deeper understanding of spirit as it operates in our daily lives. Using this, I sensed someone speaking to me and I intuitively said out loud: 'You came to me a long time ago. Now I come to you. Trust me. I am your friend. The light of the world is upon you.' I had no idea what this meant.

I decided to investigate Aura Soma further, and in the summer of 1997, I went to Lincolnshire, the home of Aura Soma, and did my first course. I learnt that your eyes are the mirror of your soul, and that you are the colours you choose. You choose four bottles that you are drawn to, and depending on the colour and position, you are given a story of yourself and where you are at that time. I learnt that I was a Divine Being of Light and a child of God.

Vicki Wall, although blind, said it was like hands were guiding her as she collected the plants and crystals to make up these bottles. As a young woman, she had trained as a pharmacist, and had devoted her life to God.

There were so many students who had done so many more spiritual things than me. They talked about higher beings, angels, archangels, and masters. I had no idea if I could cope with all this and on that first day, I lost it and cried and said I just couldn't cope. Strangely I felt I knew all about it but yet I knew nothing. It turned out others felt the same, and the teacher said I was the teacher that had come there to teach others.

So that week was for me and my growth. I opened up about my life experiences from my childhood, my abuse, and why I didn't like my name. Years later, I discovered that my 'dad' was not my father. Strangely, I had had no real connection to him or his family and I didn't like him as he had abused me from the age of nine until I left home at eighteen. Colour showed me all that I'd suffered from a child through to my adult life. By the end of the week, I felt I had achieved something for me; the first thing I had really done for myself.

In the middle of the week we used a pomander to clean and cleanse our auric field, as we did every day. We used the quintessence to connect to the Divine within us. As I stood there in my own space, I saw behind me the mouth of a cave in darkness; in front of me I saw nothing but light. It was a very profound moment for me, as I saw all the darkness I had been through and could now move more into the light. I felt I was being kicked out into the world of holistics to help others as I had been helped.

During the mediation on the last day, as we came to the end the teacher started to chant. As the chanting went on, my energy changed and I found it hard to open my eyes. I thought if I changed my breathing it would go away. Everyone else had started to chatter. I saw a bright golden light like the Sun hammering on my eyelids, and I tried to say what was needing to be said but no one was listening. The teacher gently got me to come back. For the rest of the day, I was on my own and no one really talked to me. I felt ostracized.

When we were given our certificate at the end of the day, mine was on the top. The teacher said 'Oh yes, that reminds me. I spoke with the director at lunch time and I have to tell you, we do not channel at aura soma.' And yet we all knew that Vicki Wall had channelled the knowledge about the bottles (and this was still being channelled by another as she had passed on), but we were not allowed to do it. All I had worked for during this week was taken away with a few words about what not to do, yet I hadn't asked for it, it just came. I had no idea who or what it was. Some said I should have told it to go away but it was not that easy; they did not understand how it was, or how they had treated me. The energy I felt was very strong and very powerful. But I went on to do more courses, up to teacher level 1, and helped many people come to terms with what was happening to them.

One of the most profound bottles I used was B40 Gold/Red 'I AM.' This bottle is about the energy of wisdom and gives a sense of expansion to help you express the wisdom within, to open to oneself within oneself. I had to apply it to my feet and also on my abdomen. The mixture of energies goes direct into the lymphatic system and the blood stream, creating balance where it is needed. What happened to me was a growth appeared in the bottle, and I understood later that I had removed a growth from my body; what happens in the bottle is what's happening in the body. I took Aura Soma colour into my work place and people were fascinated by the colours and I did short readings for them.

In 1999, we went to Malta on holiday, and we were invited into the house I used to live in as a child and where the abuse began. When we got home, I got up to go to work one morning and I completely fell apart. At that moment I knew which bottle. Wisdom Rescue B90. This was about living my life from a new perspective; and to access the wisdom that had always been within me and to correct the imbalance from within. The journey with Aura Soma is gentle and subtle, you hardly know it's working till you feel different.

Over the next few years, I returned again to Reiki, which offered me more healing, as well as discovering the phytobiophysics flower formulae, another colour system. With these and other experiences, I became more in tune with what I needed and who I was; my heart healed and I was able to unlock the door I had shut my whole life. I wrote a very thoughtful letter to the man who'd been my dad; he passed away soon after, and ultimately I received his apology via Spirit.

It took forty-one years to heal my physical health issues, and heal the pain and trauma of the abuse I had been through. As I look back over the years, I can see that I have come a very long way. I have come to understand that everything happens for a reason, it was all a part of my learning process to be here to help and support others to heal and grow.

I shall be forever grateful to my husband for being my catalyst, to Kate for introducing me to colour, and for the loving support I have received over the years from various people. But most of all for the God within, and the still small voice that I didn't listen to at first, but do now.

Alwyn lives on the Wirral peninsula in northern England, where she is a colour practitioner and Reiki teacher. In her spare time, she likes to travel, sew, and make healing cards.

Philippa Bennett

From Grief to Gratitude: Transforming Pain into Power

My story begins at the end. Which is not yet the end of course, but is the here and now. To say that I live in joy, freedom, and appreciation every day would of course be a lie. But the last twenty years have taken me to the point where I can and do practice appreciation daily. And while I do have bad days, I live most of the time in love, joy, and satisfaction.

Every good marketer will tell you that you are your own ideal customer, and that every good story has a beginning, a middle, and an end. So how did I get from Cornish farm girl, to gibbering wreck, to happy, balanced homeopath in the so far, short years of my life?

I was an angry child. And I mean really angry. I screamed, and threw things, and broke windows in fits of rage. I remember being pinned to the ground by my 6'4" father so that the tornado inside me wouldn't destroy a room, and I carried that rage with me well into my twenties. The journey from rage-filled farm girl to happy homeopath began in February 2000 at the invincible age of twenty-three.

I was sitting at home one night and the phone rang. I answered and a woman asked to speak to my boyfriend, J. I asked who it was, but didn't really catch the name so just handed over the phone. For the next two hours I remember every second as if it were burnt onto my retinas. I couldn't really put into words how J's face looked as he listened to the voice down the phone line. I've never really seen anything like it since. I felt the energy coming off him and I started to shake, violently. I didn't know what had happened, but I could feel it was big. Really big.

J got off the phone. I spoke first. "It's dad, isn't it?" I don't know how, but I knew. "He's killed himself, hasn't he?" J nodded.

Dad and I had always had a special bond. He was always the voice of reason when Mum and I were fighting. He understood and respected me. I couldn't believe that he was no longer physically there.

My body took over and I fitted. The emotion was more than I've ever felt, before or after. It was huge. I writhed in emotional agony, letting every breath and sound that wanted out, out.

After the beast had calmed, and I'd punched the wall a few times, I said, "I have to go to Mum." I didn't know if she was alone, or what was really going on, and although we'd never had a close relationship, my first instinct was to protect her.

We drove to Mum's. There was of a house full of neighbours all making cups of tea and shaking their heads in disbelief. And there was my mum, pacing the room until I arrived. I took her in my arms and she'd never felt so small.

To say I didn't handle the following few years well, would be an understatement. I had grown up in a very alcohol-fuelled household. We'd lived in a pub until I was six, and my father was an alcoholic. He wasn't a violent man—the opposite in fact. But he was never happier than with a pint in his hand. He was a happy and loving drunk and a loving and supportive father. He was my hero. But being a happy drunk by no means pays the bills, and he was less than good at handling money. If it was in his pocket, it was soon in the till at the pub.

So, in the name of genetics, I followed suit. For the first six months of dad-less life, I partied hard. Raves, drugs, drinking, anything to not have to deal with emotion. It was easier that way. I could have a good time, not have to process the sadness and grief, and looked like I was doing okay in the process.

After those initial six months, I couldn't take the banality of the work/partying/misery balance anymore, and so J and I decided to move to Lanzarote in Spain.

I know now that I was just chasing happiness around the planet. Wherever you go in life, you always take yourself with you. So if yourself is full of unprocessed grief and trauma, wherever you go and whatever you do, whomever you are with, it's still there, biting at your ankles, waiting for you to trip up.

Lanzarote was supposed to be a change for the good, a chance to experience another culture, get some sun and sand, and escape the free-party scene that we were so deeply ensconced in. But it just turned out to be different beer and different drugs with different people, with the sole advantage of a dip in the sea to cure the hangover. I worked hard—six days a week, nine hours a day, as a waitress, in the blazing sun, and I was damn good at it. But nothing lasts. The restaurant downscaled, and as I was last in, I was first out and subsequently jobless.

I wasn't really sure what I was going to do, but in true spirit I just continued to party. I had broken up with J and was drinking a lot. It was on one of those long, booze-fuelled evenings that I met a guy from Hamburg. He was odd. Gregarious, loud, a bit weird, but engaging and enlightened. We drank the rest of my money, I lost my flat, and we ended up sleeping in a wind-surf sail bag on the beach for two months, with the occasional overnighter in a mutual friend's garage if the weather was too cold.

I was homeless and without any direction. The rest of my money ran out and the German went back to Hamburg. But before he left, he suggested I come and live with him, and with no job, no prospects, no money, and no hope, I said yes. I had no idea how I was going to get to Hamburg from Lanzarote and my friends could see that it probably wasn't a good idea anyway, so a girlfriend gave me the money for a flight back to the UK and I went back to my mum, somewhat beaten, but determined to get to Hamburg.

It didn't go well with Mum. She was still deep in her own grief, and after a few short weeks, a very large phone bill, and many fights later, Mum put me on a bus starting in Cornwall and ending in Hamburg with £500 in my pocket.

Cutting a long story short, the boozing continued, the German didn't. I met an Aussie guy, moved to Australia, moved back to Hamburg, and back to Australia again, where we ended up living in the outback in a small town on the north-west coast of Western Australia called Kalbarri.

All those moves, and all that running away, and the pain was still there. Nothing was ever right. I was never really satisfied. There was always something else that I wanted. Always something not right with the relationship, the house, the life, the friends. But at least I was a long way from home and my mum, so I didn't have to face the feelings they brought with them.

And then, I watched *The Secret*. Yes, I know—cliché—but that's how the recovery started. I watched it again and again. I wrote journals and lists and letters to the universe and my life started to shift. I started to understand the concept that what you put out into the world, is what you get back. And that all the anger and grief I was carrying around with me, only multiplied with the energy I gave to it. By pushing it down and ignoring it, by drinking it away and running from my feelings, all I had done was make it bigger and blacker than it ever deserved to be, when love and acceptance were the healing energies I needed. I wrote to my mum and explained and apologised. I knew that I wanted to go back home. Back to Cornwall and back to where the pain began. I wanted to face it head on. I was ready and able.

So in May 2011, back to Cornwall we went.

On that list to the universe was a house in the countryside and we had it. A beautiful, draughty and damp old 1930s cottage, with a big garden and spectacular views over the rolling hills of Cornwall. The satisfaction was creeping in.

I had kept the job I had in Australia and was merrily working from home, earning good money, working good hours, and life was tickety-boo. Most of it anyway. But I knew I didn't want to sit behind a computer for the rest of my life building spreadsheets and making money for other people. But what could I do, how could I help others like me?

I had used homeopathy for fourteen years by this point and had always been amazed by its results. It had worked for me when no doctors' creams or potions could and I loved the process of the consultation. I searched around for courses and found one an hour's drive from me with, as it turned out, my own homeopath from fourteen years earlier. My homeopathic journey and climb to daily appreciation and love began.

When I started to study homeopathy, several of the senior students warned me and my fellow first years that life would never be the same again. Changes would happen that no one could ever really prepare you for, and how right they were!

I started to study and I started to see the scope of how these tiny little pills could stimulate such powerful responses. I started to feel the black, sludgy, toxic ball of grief, lurking deep inside my guts start to move and soften. I went back into my own homeopathic process, being prescribed for, and then life turned upside down. Just as they said it would.

My relationship ended. I was alone on the edge of a black hole, but homeopathy pulled me back. I knew what to do. Relationship breakups also involve the grief process and I was able to see there was a process to follow and a way out.

On my list to the universe was a happy, harmonious and affectionate relationship – the one I'd been in wasn't. As I researched more into the Law of Attraction, and discovered (or attracted into my life) the teachings of Abraham Hicks, I realised that a new relationship would be with whoever I attracted into my life.

I'd never really believed in the concept of a heaven and hell and the Christian faith I was brought up in never fit with my somewhat pagan view of life. I could always feel the power of nature and somehow intrinsically knew that we were all connected. Even from a young age, I had always felt that death was a purely physical action and that energy never really dies. After listening to Abraham a lot, this view was confirmed and I learnt at an even deeper level how the way you think, and the way you feel, make ripples into your world, which come back at you with the same, if not, more intense energy. By being mindful of my thoughts and giving love to something which all logic says I should hate, its power over me dissipated and I started to respect and love my father for his decision.

Although I was living in Cornwall again, I was visiting Hamburg regularly and had a warm and fun-loving circle of friends there. While sitting at the bar in my friends' pub (alcohol was still a big part of my life), in walked a man who I would spend the next seven plus years with. It's still going strong. List item: happy, harmonious, affectionate relationship. Check!

I still had two years until my homeopathic study was finished so I commuted monthly between Cornwall and Hamburg, learning what it was like to have fun and be happy, and not feeling like I was lugging around a heavy weight of grief in my guts. I was still drinking too much, more because of the social situation than anything else. Life was very pub-based, but I worked, and studied and qualified.

At this point I was pretty content. I had a good qualification under my belt and a great partner by my side, but I knew there was more to reach for. By then I hadn't listened to Abraham Hicks for a while, and as soon as the thought came into my head that it was my desire to reach for more and more satisfaction, up popped their videos on my YouTube feed. I started absorbing daily snippets and journaling my lists of positive aspects.

I have always had a bit of a fascination with ghosts and ghouls. I've had a few weird interactions with unexplained phenomena over the years and I'd always hoped that one day I would somehow see or feel my Dad. Although I had come to accept his decision and grown to appreciate the good that came out of his actions, the niggling question of 'why' had long been at the back of my mind.

I came to realise that he, as well as every loved one I've ever lost or anyone I've ever known who has passed, is all around me, all the time. Abraham talks a lot about dreams and how when you dream of a passed love one, they are just making contact to check how you're doing. This felt so right to me and I very often dream of my grand-parents, with whom I was very close.

Then one day, after a particularly good meditation, I was sitting eating breakfast and I suddenly felt my Dad. He was such a huge man and he always had a very distinctive smell. He worked hard and would often come home dirty and sweaty and I really loved as a child how comforting it felt to know he was home. Over that piece of post-meditation toast, I could feel and smell him. And it was wonderful. I know without a shadow of a doubt, that he's happy and content, watching over me at every step of the way, in the collective energetic soup which makes up our universe.

The question of 'why' just feels so irrelevant now. And through mindful focus, and regular meditation, my appreciation, perspective, and satisfaction have reached new levels. And now this angry Cornish farm girl rarely gets angry at all. I never feel depression. I never lose myself in rage. Most days, I wake up feeling ready and inspired and motivated. I love being in the countryside and I no longer feel fear of the unexpected. I know that everything will be alright and that everything that comes to me is for the greater good.

Grief locked me in an uncomfortable cage, but love and appreciation set me free. The journey is by no means finished. There are things to do, people to help, love to give. But my spiritual transformation has been the best thing that happened to me, and I feel sure it wouldn't have happened if my dad hadn't left the movie early. I love him even more because of it.

I believe we evolved on this earth, in this galaxy, in our universe, to be happy. I believe the miracle of our birth is so we can do great things and enjoy this amazing planet. Some people forget this, some don't realise this, or just don't want to realise this and think that life happens to them, instead of because of them. I thought that too. I thought that my life was a mess, because other people ruined it with their actions. But happiness comes from within, and if you can express love from within, in any given situation, you've cracked the code. I'm still working on it.

Philippa is a Well-being Therapist, living on the Baltic coast of Northern Germany. In her spare time she enjoys live-music concerts and gardening.

Karolyn McPherson

It's all a question of perspective

My story is about the balance of light and dark, recognising and accepting these aspects of myself, releasing fear of my darker side, knowing that this and the choices I have made, have formed the person I am today.

As a teenager, I felt a lot of anger and frustration. I loved to watch horror movies (encouraged by my grandmother), although they terrified me. I was fascinated with all things mystical, reading books about magic and the occult. One night my friend and I, in our naive curiosity, decided to try out an ouija board. When the glass began to rapidly fly across the board, disbelief turned to shock and fear and we poured water in the glass, burned the paper, and never discussed it until many years later. Around this time, my brother and I had disagreements, sometimes escalating into physical brawls resulting in ornaments and even glass panelled doors being smashed in the process. I remember shaking with anger, and then later on, after calming down, I felt ashamed and remorseful. There was a specific incident during a fight when a heavy wardrobe fell, nearly landing on him. I couldn't explain why it had fallen but I had a sense it was due to my anger. I was extremely grateful he wasn't harmed and remember thinking it was somehow related to the ouija experience. I recited the Lord's prayer and asked that I be released from any evil attachments so no harm would come to my brother or anyone else because of this or my emotions. The experiences disturbed me greatly and I made a choice to turn away from this destructive path and began exploring religion. First, I attended the local church where my grandpa and mum were members. Although the minister was a lovely grandfatherly figure, I found the sermons dull and the hymns dreary. I joined a friend a few times attending her church and I really enjoyed the joyous uplifting singing but was unwilling to adhere to what I considered to be restrictive rules and judgemental opinions. I concluded that I didn't need to go to church to pray, and that spirituality was more about behaviour and acts of kindness, not judgement of, or trying to impose beliefs on, others. I still believe in these principles today.

My first experience of Reiki was receiving a healing from a friend's mother after being injured on a skiing holiday. I had never heard of Reiki and agreed to the treatment mainly out of curiosity. I didn't believe it would make a difference but thought what harm can it do.

I was surprised when Hannah told me where the pain was as I hadn't told her the full extent. I rationalised that the improvement in how I felt was coincidental because I had no other logical explanation.

After returning from holiday, when a friend mentioned she was going to see a Reiki master, I was intrigued and asked to join her. It seemed an unusual coincidence that the subject had arisen in such quick succession, having known nothing of it previously. Roberta was instantly likeable, although I thought her a little eccentric. I felt uncharacteristically comfortable and found myself telling her personal details about feelings and experiences previously unshared, and certainly not with a relative stranger.

After spending time learning more about Reiki and its origins, I felt open to working with this healing energy for myself. I had an attunement to Reiki level one later that afternoon. During the attunement I felt a comforting warmth flowing through me and I saw beautiful vibrant purple colours and the shape of a man with the head of an elephant, later discovering it was Ganesh. In retrospect I believe he came forward to help me remove internal obstacles: my closed ego mind, cynicism, and being able to get out of my own head.

The shell necklace I was wearing became so hot that I had to remove it. Roberta told me I had a dragon with me and the heat was a result of its energy being released. I didn't understand, even telling, her that I didn't believe in weird witchy stuff. Those exact words have often been reflected back at me over the years since, the humour of which isn't lost on me. However, the dragon resonated with me, often having dreamt of dragons and having had a fascination with them since childhood. Somehow this felt right. From that day onwards, my connection with dragons and their energy has grown stronger, they continue to appear to me in dreams, and when I am meditating or doing distance healing; they are my guardians and spiritual guides. Years later, when I did a course in dragon Arcturian light healing, I dreamt about specific dragons and their energies before my teacher had sent out the pre-class information. I was able to describe them in great detail, so much so that she ended up changing the planned lessons, asking which dragon I had connected with and then going with them.

The night after my initial attunement to reiki I felt much

lighter and a sense of elation, although my analytical mind couldn't grasp what had happened. Over the next few weeks, I experienced heightened feelings; I felt energy flowing from my hands, especially near close friends and family, dreams were more vivid, and I'd hear from people as I was thinking of them, and even discovered that some of the dreams had transpired.

I continued trying to convince myself that this was all just coincidence, until one day, when out with a friend, I had a sudden onset of back and leg pain. My hands became really hot and were tingling with energy. Instinctively I felt the pain was hers, and I sheepishly asked if she was experiencing back and leg pain which she confirmed. She then went on to surprise me by saying "you're doing Reiki!" It transpired that a few weeks earlier she had been for a Reiki treatment. Finally, I conceded that this was no longer coincidence. I didn't understand how it worked but I accepted that it undoubtedly did. The experience was the catalyst for me to continue on my spiritual path. The more I worked with the energies and tuned in to my inner voice, the stronger the energies felt. It was essentially exercising and honing my spiritual connection.

I trusted more in my intuition, and acknowledged and accepted that this was a gift, and I stopped feeling afraid of the judgement of others and what they might think of me. I accept others as they are and respect their beliefs regardless of whether I share them; others opinions of me are just that: theirs alone, not something I am responsible for. Realising this, and that I deserved the same respect in return, and releasing that weight, was very freeing. Soon after I went on to be attuned at Reiki 2 level, then later Reiki master teacher.

Along with my fulltime job in the NHS, I did healings for

friends, family, work colleagues, and pets and animals—two of my cats living until almost 20, something I attribute to their regular Reiki treatments. I studied and sat many exams furthering my career and gaining promotion. However, I forgot the most important part of Reiki, taking time for myself and self-love. I was too busy for me, always putting others before myself.

My work environment changed dramatically and I was promoted to area manager. The relationship with my manager was tense; I found her to be confrontational, volatile, verbally aggressive, sometimes even physically violent lashing out at equipment. I found her behaviour difficult to deal with and mostly I'd remain quiet until I felt her calm down, or I'd try to avoid her completely, choosing to communicate electronically.

Things began to spiral with increasing pressure, staff shortages due to sickness, patient complaints regarding staff, and a major traffic route was closed causing significant disruption to travel and travel time increased from one hour to three hours each way. Not surprisingly, health issues arose; fibroids caused such heavy bleeding that I became anaemic resulting in breathlessness and lethargy. I continued doing my job to the best of my ability, daily practising setting up auric protection, but no self-healing or self-care. In my mind I had no time or energy for hobbies outside work. I'd work late to get everything done, missing dance and exercise classes with my husband because of it. I felt overwhelmed, and physically and mentally exhausted. I withdrew from family and friends. I was hospitalised due to urinary retention, something I'd had a couple of warning issues over but put off dealing with because my work came first and I was too busy. I even tried to organise the department from my hospital bed until the surgeon threatened to take my phone away if I didn't stop. I now clearly see how low my self-worth and self-love were. Hindsight is a wonderful thing.

It took my GP telling me that my blood pressure was so high that I could have a stroke, and signing me off work, for me to finally leave the situation. My parents didn't want me to leave the well-paid job; they have always expected that I should excel in exams, push through illness when at school, then work regardless. It's not in their nature to give praise no matter what, although I guess it's something I have always sought. I felt I was a failure, that I'd let them down, but my life was much more important than any job.

Within a few weeks in the new job, my blood pressure returned to normal, the medication put me into menopause, stopping the bleeding and resolving the anaemia. I practised gratitude every morning as soon as I woke up, something that has continued ever since. I remembered and began practising all of the Reiki principles, first and foremost self-love and self-care. Within the first few weeks I met and immediately connected with two beautiful souls, forming a strong bond and becoming spiritual mentor and close friends with them. I was appreciated by colleagues. It was a clear revelation that what I was putting out energetically was coming back to me.

I was at work on my birthday, and colleagues gave me cards, gifts, cake, and sang *happy birthday* to me. It was a lovely day, and I felt loved, and greatly appreciated all of their kindness and well wishes. On leaving work, a colleague from the previous job messaged me wishing me a happy birthday, asking how my day had been, I replied "I've had a lovely day, and I've been spoiled by my colleagues" She replied: Bastards!" Her response took me aback until I realised she'd interpreted it negatively assuming I meant 'spoilt' as in 'ruined.' Another lightbulb moment for me. I was responsible for creating my own reality. Gratitude, perspective, self-love, and compassion are key.

Karolyn lives in Polmont, Scotland, and works in the NHS as a sonographer. She is a reiki master and works with the energy of crystals, especially crystal dragons and skulls. In her spare time, she's a keen amateur photographer and enjoys belly dancing and ballroom dancing.

Joanne Bracken

Singing Myself Free

When I was seven years old and a second grader in elementary school, I adopted the strange notion that I wanted to be a saint when I grew up. How did I ever get that idea into my head? Other children were out catching frogs, playing hopscotch, and trying to stay out of trouble. Not me. I already knew deep inside that there was another option, one that I could surely qualify for at some point in my life. I just had to follow the teachings of the Catholic Church, live a pure life, and make Jesus my focus.

My first holy communion came the same year, and all I wanted was to be the bride of Christ. I realize now that my preoccupation with holiness was the beginning of my life journey toward enlightenment. What I did not fully understand then was that all the saints suffered tremendously. Over the years, I read several stories of the lives of the saints, and they were usually tortured and killed or died difficult deaths through illness. These people earned sainthood because of their unwavering devotion to God as they suffered.

Suffering was a foundation of my upbringing. My family was highly dysfunctional, my father being a sick, alcoholic abuser. My siblings and I lived in fear of a father who was angry, unpredictable, shaming, and physically and mentally abusive. My mother, afraid for her own safety, turned away and pretended everything was good enough at home. Besides, divorce was out of the question for Catholics, and she did not have the money to go out on her own with four children.

During the darkest of times as a teenager, I had several dreams in which Mother Mary appeared, offering nurturing and love through her presence rather than any words spoken. From the time I learned about Mary at school, I felt a deep, loving bond with her. I know now that she came to help me navigate through the family trauma. When I was sixteen, I thought about suicide because there was no other way to escape; I know that Mary's presence lifted me up and provided care and support which I was not receiving in any measure from my family. Through some means that I did not understand, she imbued me with a sense of hope that better days would come, even though it did not seem possible from my vantage point then.

During these tumultuous years, I found solace in singing. When I was particularly upset, I'd close myself in my room and play my records, singing along with artists I felt were my personal friends – Joni Mitchell, Judy Collins, The Carpenters, The Mamas and the Papas, John Denver, and others. I could shift my mood so easily; it was a brilliant method of self-healing, as the musical frequencies wrapped me in a cocoon of sound like a warm, sonic massage. Little did I know then the power of this exercise or that I would expand on this later in life.

After a decade of intense emotional turmoil and depression, directly related to the abuse I suffered from my father, a new path opened before me. In August 1972, my mother discovered an audition notice in our local newspaper calling for local singers for a production of *The Mikado* by Gilbert and Sullivan. She cut it out for me, thinking that it would be something that would lift my spirits. I had never done anything musical other than sing with my high school glee club for four years, which I loved; I'm sure singing carried me through my pain. I am amazed now that I mustered up enough courage to audition for this show, but my soul was clearly leading me on an exciting new adventure. I was accepted into the company as a soprano chorister and soon after that I joined a church choir. So began a new decade of expansion through vocal and theatrical performance. Suddenly I had lots of new friends and an outlet for my creativity.

For ten years, performing with local troupes and choirs was my passion. I thrived on the schedule of rehearsals, performances, and social gatherings that jammed my calendar. In addition to all these activities, I also worked full-time, but I was young and loved the constant busyness, doing what I loved with a whole new group of friends and colleagues that brought a level of joy that I had not experienced before.

As I grew closer to age thirty, I started to notice that I did not feel as excited about all my musical activities and was growing tired of the schedule and began to drop some commitments. Singing became more of a chore than something that gave me pleasure. Also, I experienced a difficult period with my health which led to me having a hysterectomy at age twenty-seven. This was a tremendous blow because I had always wanted marriage and children, and this was not in the picture yet. I went through terrible depression, forced to re-examine what my life was about and where I would be heading. It was a devastating time, made even worse by my youngest sister's marriage and arrival of her first baby. I tried to be happy for her, but my own suffering over my loss made expressing joy for my sister extremely challenging. I felt damaged, broken, unloved, and insignificant.

What was I going to do with my life? I did not know where I fit in anymore. I was thrown into the deepest period of self-examination I had yet known. Some people describe it as "the dark night of the soul." I entered a space of emptiness, a void, waiting for something to be illuminated so that I knew which path to follow. While sitting in that uncomfortable hole, I did what was in front of me – I went to work and partied with friends. I had great fun, but something big was missing. I kept asking, "What's next?" and waited for the answer to be revealed. My life seemed superficial and meaningless, so I focused on having as much fun as possible to distract me from a deep sense of emptiness.

My spiritual side used to be so important to me, but it took a back seat during the years when I was involved in musical activities and boyfriends. I seemed to have forgotten about my love of the Divine. The little girl who dreamed of sainthood had grown into a working woman who loved to party with friends after hours and engage in more normal activities. However, the underlying thread of love of the metaphysical was satisfied occasionally by going to a downtown restaurant that featured psychics who read Tarot cards. My friends and I also enjoyed many evenings working with a Ouija Board. I had no idea what I was doing and did not know anything about protecting myself in the process. I count myself lucky to have avoided any negative visitations by less than friendly spirits.

Soon after my hysterectomy, I had the feeling that a deep, internal switch got flipped. I was in my late twenties with no marriage prospects and no ability to have children of my own. Music performance had moved to the background in my experience. I still sang for myself in the quiet of my home, allowing the vibrations of my own voice to soothe and uplift me, but I moved away from the group activities. In this latest experience of stillness and reflection, I started to question everything about my life and where I fit in the world. What was my purpose? My metaphysical interests started moving to the forefront of my awareness, but not as a game now. I started devouring books on spirituality and healing which took me out of the pain and depression of my current loss and lack of direction.

Once again, when I needed a sense of purpose and my own value in the world, a new path showed itself. One day during my lunch hour at work, I walked up a short, narrow street into the little town that had become the center of my world as a young working professional. I had been up that street many times but did not remember ever seeing this amazing little shop before. As I approached the entrance, I noticed the engraved name on the glass window—*The Avant Garde Bookstore and Study Center*. My heart leapt, and I felt excitement instantly bubble up in me. I went in and felt like I had suddenly entered a magical garden of otherworldly delights.

As I looked over all the shelves of books on multitudes of spiritual topics – crystals, New Age music tapes, Tarot decks, and much more – I was full of wonder that such a place existed. *Avante Garde* had been in this location for a few years, but I had been oblivious to its existence until now. It was time to crawl out of my dark hole and enter a new journey of self-discovery that would set the stage for the rest of my life.

Hungry for everything that *Avante Garde* had to offer, I began to take classes in psychic development, Tarot card reading, past-life regression, and different energy healing modalities. I was in a constant state of joy and excitement and felt that I had returned home in some way. Pursuing the spiritual arts awakened something in me that felt familiar and ancient. Clearly, I had been guided to this magical place to discover hidden treasures within me, such as my talent for giving readings; I was soon one of the store's regular Tarot readers. I felt that my life had meaning and purpose as I got busy giving readings and continuing my training as a healer and intuitive reader.

My discovery of the bookstore and all it offered for my spiritual development provided a portal into what I would call my Divine Blueprint or the path that I was always meant to follow. Over the last three decades, I have developed my skills in healing and spiritual counseling and have a practice today that feeds me.

There is, however, one part of my life that I could never get together in the way I wished – intimate partnerships. I have never experienced a genuinely loving relationship, and I am sure that is because I grew up without having love and tenderness at home. How do you learn what real love is when you have never had an appropriate role model? Finding love escaped me, and I found myself drawn to men who were much like my father: narcissistic, abusive, and emotionally unavailable.

Success came to me in my ability to build a healing practice while also working full-time, but I deeply longed to experience a loving partnership. The few men I dated quickly became emotionally abusive, and the relationships died out within a year. I did not understand why love escaped me, especially when people kept telling me what a good person I was, and a man would be lucky to have me. I thought I was not good enough. What is missing in me that makes finding love so unattainable? The people in my life who should have been supportive and nurturing, including family, friends, boyfriends, and neighbors, regularly criticized my looks; I was criticized for being too fat, too flat-chested, too tall, and I had skinny legs. While I longed to feel love and acceptance, I did not have it for myself because I believed what I was told.

Because of these betrayals, I have been extremely cautious about sharing my heart. It has been smashed too many times. In 1993, I found a man who seemed to be a good fit, and I married him in 1995, but he too turned out to be a bad match. He turned into my father, becoming nasty, abusive, and critical of me soon after we married. He also started drinking heavily. I felt I had come full circle in one respect; at the age of forty-two, I was shocked into the awareness that I was living with my father again, suffering similar mental abuse and diving into depression as I wondered what happened. I really thought I was done with my father stuff. But what I had now, which I did not have as a child, was choice. I could choose to stay in this situation and suffer, or end it.

A spiritual counselor at that time said something powerful to me that was like a lightning bolt to my consciousness. She said, "You will never heal your relationship with your father by being married to another sick man." Wow. That was a gut-punch, for sure. I stuck with this man until it became intolerable, divorcing him in 1997. The day he left was one of the happiest days of my life. It was time to reclaim myself, rebuild my confidence, and undertake another deep dive into my psyche and all the programming and beliefs I had about my value. I began to examine what self-love and unconditional self-acceptance meant and how I would develop these qualities in myself. I began to understand that, in order to experience genuine love from a partner, I needed to give that to myself. It is such a simple concept but by no means an easy thing to master. So I consciously swore off dating until I got right with myself.

My life has seemed like a jumble of experiences that have drawn on different aspects of my soul, whether performer, teacher, or healer. Intimate relationships have been a disappointing side bar, and yet the way my close relationships have played out has been so important to examine as part of my earthly journey. While the relationship issue is still a work in progress, I am expressing the healer that I am in a beautiful way. In the late-1980s, I wondered if there was a way that my love of singing and healing could be used together. Surely my musical experience was not a waste.

In the early 1990s, I was introduced to the science and practice of sound healing, and it excited me beyond measure. Sound healing became my new passion, and I was enthralled with how we could shift energy when using various vocal sounds. Living in Boulder, Colorado in 1993, I discovered a world-renowned sound healer and composer, Jonathan Goldman, who lived within a few miles of me. Jonathan offered local workshops which I feel blessed to have attended. Jonathan's workshops, held in a beautiful natural setting surrounded by forests and mountains, allowed me to make the connection for myself in how to use my vocal gifts in healing body, mind, and spirit. Joining with a hundred other sound enthusiasts was a truly ecstatic experience, a form of heaven on earth. I experienced singing, toning, and chanting as a gateway to connection with the God at a level I could never have imagined.

Working with sacred sound has opened my heart in a way that nothing else has done in the past. It has allowed me to see and experience fully the gifts that I am here to express. The more I engage in sacred sound practice and meditation, the deeper my connection with Spirit and my authentic self, and the freer I become. More and more, I can detach from the old programming of my early years and experience myself as a spark of divinity. Gone is the child who dreamed of being a saint, and a woman has taken her place who knows her value simply because she is a unique expression of divinity and the love of the Supreme Creator. Suffering is no longer a goal but rather finding joy in allowing the divine to shine through me and my experiences. I much prefer this way of being.

Joanne Bracken lives on the East Coast of the USA with her sweet feline companion, Micah. Joanne is a sound healer, channeler, and past-life therapist. In her spare time, she enjoys get-togethers with friends, walks in nature, and attending concerts.

Alison Kerr

Learning to see myself through eyes of love

Although I started on my spiritual/healing path twenty years ago, I've only fully started to understand myself, and by default other humans, in the past couple of years.

I was brought up in Glasgow, Scotland, and my background is that of a dysfunctional family, with a lot of physical and psychological abuse. I spent the first thirty years of my life feeling less than, not good enough, bad, unworthy, and not feeling as though I fitted in despite outward appearances. I was attractive, intelligent, popular, did well at school, and had a good secure job. However, from as early as primary school I was belted, given punishment lines to write, and made to stand in the corner of the classroom facing the wall. I was clearly acting out, but getting further punishment at school rather than support. By fifteen, I was smoking cigarettes and drinking, and I later progressed to other drugs. It's only in later life that I realised that I had spent most of my life in a state of anxiety, with bouts of depression, and that the drugs helped with that. Every action has a positive intention. Drink and drugs helped me to feel less anxious, more confident, and more able to connect with others, something I was desperately seeking due to the lack of emotional connection at home. I had no understanding at the time that my parents were abusive and I certainly had no idea that I was an empath or what that meant. I just knew that I was called 'too touchy' when I got upset at teasing or criticism. Reading *Psychic Empath,*[10] I discovered that it's not uncommon for empaths to numb their overwhelming feelings with drink and drugs.

I spent much of my life thinking there has to be more to life than this, and my biggest fear as I grew up was to spend my whole life without reaching my full potential. As I got older, I realised that the fear was actually of not achieving my life purpose, and it grew more urgent over the years.

After a failed marriage at thirty, I was in a relationship with an English-born Muslim who was a beautiful, gentle soul. However, my parents, who were racist, homophobic, and narrow minded, like many of their generation, and didn't even meet this man who was a big part of my life for several years. In fact, my dad disowned me, for the second time, over my choice of partner.

My partner's father was equally unimpressed, and the disapproval of our parents helped to push us to the divinely inspired decision to travel to Australia. I felt the most excited and alive I had felt in a long time or perhaps even ever. The fourteen months we spent there were among the best of my life. Getting away from my family, I started to discover who I really was, outside of their labels, criticism, and judgements.

While in Australia, in 1999, I was introduced to reiki. This was the start. Prior to this I had always been interested in fortune tellers. Psychic ability ran in my family although it was of no interest to them. I was the one who was fascinated

---

[10] Jason Dyer, 2019

by it and yet I couldn't do it, which was a great frustration to me over the years.

While on the beach alone one morning, feeling unwell, I was approached by a fellow Glaswegian who said she was drawn to speak to me. When I mentioned feeling unwell, she offered me a reiki treatment, which I accepted, as I had heard about reiki but had never experienced it and was curious. When I expressed my interest in learning reiki, she became my first teacher. I didn't fully understand where this healing energy came from. Reiki, roughly translated, means universal life force, and it made sense that if God created the universe, then he also created this energy. My idea of God at that time was learned through Sunday school classes at a Protestant church and I thought of 'him' as a judgemental being who would punish wrongdoings.

My reiki journey continued when I came home to Glasgow in January 2000 when I met my next reiki teacher in the first job that I took. She trained me to practitioner level and I continued to learn and started to get results with others. When a woman came to our office to get advice on setting up her own reiki practice, I finally noticed that reiki kept appearing in my life and realised that maybe I should pay more attention. I trained to master (teacher) level and when the office closed five years after I had started, I saw this as my opportunity to take a leap of faith and start my own business. My relationship had ended and I had money in the bank from the sale of our flat. I worked as a practitioner for a while but got the most joy and fulfilment out of teaching reiki to others. When I had worked in the bank, the area I was most interested in was training, and if I had a pound for every person over the years who asked if I was a teacher, I'd be a lot better off. Reiki opened up a whole new world for me. To promote my business, I took stalls at mind, body and soul fairs. I was like a child in a sweet shop at these events. I would always get a reading and loved to try new healing modalities or buy crystals or angel cards. It was far more than a hobby though; it was where I got my buzz. I didn't realise at the time that these things were literally raising my vibration.

As I continued with the regular reiki self-treatments, my drug-taking decreased. I believe that initially my vibration was so low that taking the drugs helped my state. However, as my vibration raised, taking drugs lowered it, making me feel worse. Reiki made me realise that there was more to life than I had been taught. I was starting to understand myself as a spiritual, energetic being. The messages from deceased loved ones that I received in readings made me believe in life after death, and when events were forecast and then came to pass, this made me believe that to an extent our paths are mapped out for us.

Over the years I read books, attended lots of workshops, and learned several different healing modalities, in a constant search to fix myself and be happy. I tried affirmations but they didn't make any difference. I tried meditation but could never get the hang of it. I attended psychic development classes but everyone else got information apart from me. It was frustrating and I would give up for a time before trying again and getting the same result.

Fast forward to a couple of years ago when the call to work as a healer/teacher became more urgent. I was thirty-nine and had stopped working in order to spend time raising my daughter. She filled a hole in my life that I didn't know was there and was one of my biggest healings. I believe that being a mother was also one of my purposes; to be a conscious mum to a conscious child. I believe she is an empath too. I took a job in an office again for the security of a guaranteed regular income, despite feeling that it was soul-destroying. The plan had been to start working for myself again when she started school. She is now fourteen and I'm only now feeling ready to do this. I was aware that time was passing and I wasn't any further on and felt pushed to learn and get a move on. I started out down the NLP route thinking this was what I needed in order to be a good coach. But then I discovered Theta healing, took my first course in February 2019, and finally found the thing that worked for me. I've never been a patient person and always like to get to the point. I don't have a lot of tolerance for faffing about and I was amazed at how quickly Theta healing changed me. In one year, I healed more than I had in the past two decades. Theta healing works by the practitioner connecting to Creator, which shifts their brain waves into the theta state. The client also shifts into theta brainwaves in resonance and this allows us to access the subconscious. With the help of Creator, we send the energy of unconditional love to the client and intuitively scan the client's body to learn where they are holding old trauma and emotions. Through questioning, we unearth unhelpful beliefs which Creator clears, and with Creator's help we then download more helpful beliefs and feelings. My understanding of Creator is now somewhat different; I believe that we are all part of the energy of creation (Creator) which is neither masculine nor feminine, and is not judgemental or punishing. I believe that when we can learn to connect to this energy all things are possible, including instant healings and the ability to manifest what we want in our lives. During the three foundation courses, I learned that I received information by feeling in my own body where my client was holding emotions or trauma in theirs. Through time and practice I also learned that I had a sense of knowing what the issue was as they were talking to me. The real turnaround came on the fifteen day intuitive anatomy course, where each day we worked on different areas of the body, learning what they represented. I learned for example that we hold trauma in our digestive system which explained my irritable bowel syndrome and lifelong constipation; I had literally been holding on to my shit! Through reiki and several books, I had gained the understanding that each illness we develop corresponds to a very specific pattern of emotional and psychological stress and that certain beliefs and attitudes influence corresponding areas of the body. By working on myself and others for that fifteen days, through all the body systems, and seeing for myself that we all held similar emotions in the same areas, I understood this on a far deeper level.

I discovered that I had learned to dissociate from my feelings from an early age as I found them too overwhelming. It was quite a challenge to surrender the barriers that I had subconsciously put in place to protect myself but I realised that these barriers, as well as helping to prevent pain, also prevented me from fully feeling the pleasure and the deep connection that I had been craving for most of my life. In one session, working on the trauma related to childhood physical and emotional abuse, I could feel the pain in my lower abdomen where I had been holding on to it; that pain left when the trauma and associated beliefs were cleared. After subsequent sessions, going deeper each time, I no longer suffer from chronic constipation. Many of my ongoing ailments are now a thing of the past. I had spent thousands of pounds on massage over the years for chronic shoulder pain but now realise that I was treating the symptom rather than the cause. The disconnection and loneliness I suffered for as long as I can remember is no longer an issue and I enjoy my own company. I learnt that the quality of our lives is determined by the quality of our relationships, and that starts with our relationship with ourselves. I now believe that my loneliness stemmed from my disconnection from self.

In the six months following the course, I worked on healing myself in order to gain clarity on my path and the confidence to set up in business. Then covid-19 lockdown came, giving me the opportunity to devote even more time to my growth, with daily meditations, weekly sessions and practice clients, online events, and lots of audio books as I took my daily walks in nature. I believe this 'pause' as a result of the virus is a spiritual awakening and I now understand the urgency to rise to the occasion. To develop my intuition, I took a tarot course, where I met a woman who did a soul plan reading for me. This told me my worldly and spiritual challenges, talents and goals. Everything in this reading was spot on. This cemented my belief that, as souls, we choose the lives we are living in order to learn and grown. With that belief, I can't blame anyone for anything that I have experienced and have to accept full responsibility. I believe we come here many times as male and female, rich and poor, healthy and unhealthy, perpetrator and victim, and lots of other contrasts, in order to evolve. I believe that someone may be a healer in many lives and that we have soul families who come with us and may or may not be involved in parts of our lives.

I have come to the conclusion that I am here as a spiritual teacher and I believe that there will be a great need for more of us as we go through this shift. I'm beginning to understand that my challenges as an anxious teen and adult, struggling with being an empath and how overwhelming I found that, are part of what I am here to teach.

After years of being hard on myself (and others) with unachievable expectations which always led to disappointment and a feeling of failure, I now see how far I have come, how much I have grown, and how much I have achieved. After years of hating myself for my imperfections, I am learning to love myself despite them, finally accepting them as part of my humanness. I'm able to let go of the shame and guilt that I have held onto for years and that has been my biggest healing. I can now look back at my life and understand the reasons for my behaviours and choices.

Now I understand that I wasn't 'too touchy' or 'too big for my boots' or many of the other things that my parents, or others, told me over the years that I accepted as fact. I realise how much of my life I spent dissociated from my body and my feelings because as an empath I found them overwhelming. I am only just fully understanding the truth about how our beliefs, thoughts, and words shape our reality; how our beliefs create our outward experience; how our emotions both 'good' and 'bad' (or less comfortable), along with pain or illness in our body, are the body's way of talking to us and letting us know there is something that we need to look at. When we fully feel our emotions, they pass through us. When we try to suppress them, they get stuck in our body, and the effects can be devastating if we ignore them for too long as they will surface in some fashion at some point when the accumulation becomes too much for our body to hold. The relief that I have felt letting go of the old beliefs, identities, and emotions has been life changing. My only regret is that it has taken me so long. However, I understand that this has been my journey, which is not over yet, and as I heal, I can recognize my gifts and talents rather than focusing on what I perceived as broken. I realise that I am here to share all that I have learned with others and to be of service to the world by teaching them the emotional understanding that I have learned, how to heal our trauma and forgive ourselves and ultimately love ourselves. Only when we heal, forgive, and love ourselves can we be the conscious creators we are here to be.

I am excited for the future, for myself, and for the planet. As we awaken and heal our trauma, what kind of world will we create? A much better one that we currently inhabit, I pray.

Alison Kerr, lives in Giffnock, Glasgow. She is a coach and enjoys walking in nature, yoga, and metaphysical pursuits.

Jude Craig

The Power of Intention

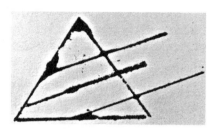

The unforgettable moments I witnessed on a small Greek island will stay with me always. So many defining decisions happened there over thirteen consecutive summers, bathed in sunshine and soaked in soul-searching. Some would call it a spiritual home, and my learnings from those deeply nourishing shores journeyed with me and so often manifested into magic.

Even now, I can feel myself gliding graciously into the pine circle where I often facilitated my complementary therapy workshops. I always noticed how much my pace slowed while on Skyros. The elongated trip from Scotland – with a train, plane, bus, ferry, and final rickety bus – afforded me time to truly arrive ready for work, rest, and play, in no particular order, resulting in annual restoration of my body, mind, and soul. I created my outdoor classroom with yoga mats scattered randomly in and out of the shade for reflexology recipients to lie on, and chairs on which the giver of reflexology would sit. It became a learning space for me to share the wonders of an ancient therapy that works with 7000 nerve endings in the feet – a welcome punctuation for these often-neglected appendages that are said to journey us twice round the world in an average life time. The group gathered daily for a couple of hours of gentle tuition, both giving and receiving therapy.

This particular experience occurred sometime before the 2001 life-changing earthquake. It was the last day of the week-long programme I had been offering. Participants were invited to offer their learned skills to another group member and swap a full reflexology session, without me interrupting to impart wisdom about this divinely holistic therapy. As I moved around the circle, I noticed an elderly lady looking slightly agitated. She looked at me and mouthed the words *I have forgotten everything, I don't know what to do* and her eyes were wide with concern. All the time she was expressing her lack of confidence, she was also squeezing and enveloping the gentleman's feet that were resting on her lap. I explained how beautifully her hands were working and reminded her of my simple 'colouring in' approach, that as long as she used touch with fingers, thumbs, and hands, to colour in every part of each foot, she would be doing really well. She settled into a way of working that looked intuitively natural.

The session time was nearing the end and partners were sitting together to offer feedback. The lady explained to her partner that she forgot what to do and I could almost hear an apology brewing in her voice. The gentleman listened to her with smiling eyes then said these words which are forever etched in my soul. "I thank you from the bottom of my heart for I have never in all my life felt so nurtured and cared for and held and you have given me the greatest gift imaginable." There was hardly a dry eye in the group, and as tears of joy rolled down my own cheeks, I realised I had witnessed a very important lesson. I learned that *what* we do is much less important than the *intention* with which we do it.

Pouring clear and positive intention into any thought or action can make all the difference. It moves us from pure skill to holding the space open for the recipient to take what they need from the opportunity. This can spill into many areas of life and work and *intention* has remained an important word and practice for me as a result of this vividly beautiful experience.

On the same trip, while I was tweaking my teaching to accommodate the development of positive intention, and exactly a lunar cycle after that enlightening moment, something strange was in the air. The animals seemed restless and unusually noisy. Dogs barked more sharply and goats' bells rang with a tempo that had moved up a pace. Cockerels' piercing cries resounded around the cove while the relentless cicadas were deafening with no respite. Cats, which were many, slunk around, stretching, seemingly more in an angry posture than happy cat mode. I had an uneasy feeling and decided to rest early in my hut. I read a little, and meditated to slip past the sounds that filled the night. I drifted into slumber.

I woke abruptly just after 3am, and felt my bed shaking and heard bits of I-don't-know-what falling off the roof. Seconds seemed like minutes and it was getting more vigorous and my head struggled to make sense of what was shaking the earth below me so roughly. People screamed and ran out of buildings and outdoor rooms; I was riveted to the spot where I lay. I repeated over and over *please let the earth stop moving now*. I heard breaking glass and stone work disintegrating, and still I lay repeating my mantra, willing the earth to stop moving. The strong rumbling vibrations felt like an upside-down thunder storm from within the earth itself. After more moments than I wished for, it ceased. A blanket of natural silence fell upon the land and sea. Not a peep from any creature great or small. Voices of various tones echoed, and I rose and went to one of the public gathering areas, as I thought the retreat community may need some support. I walked along the shore road and stared at the sea which looked like glass. Not a ripple, not a wave and not a sound. It felt eerily calm.

I found people sounding alarmed, wandering aimlessly, or huddled in small groups holding themselves together. Another earth rumble occurred and my hands and arms automatically raised from my sides in an effort to stay balanced. There were high pitch squeals, and gasps of worry that the quake would repeat or worsen, and gazes of disbelief at being in this unfamiliar territory. Everyone's eyes seemed to be darting around looking for advice on how to behave and what to do next, and it was only slightly comforting that those who lived on the island explained that there would likely be after-tremors for some time but that they were usually smaller. It was the strangest thing to have lived my life solidly on terra firma and suddenly to find myself on very shaky ground. It did indeed shake me, in several ways that unfolded over the next few days.

It was decided that those sleeping in stone buildings or in outdoor huts with concrete roofs should sleep out in the open spaces and everyone quietly went about gathering bedding, pillows, and blankets to create an alfresco place in which to be for a while. I went to pick up my nest-making materials and thought about the heavy concrete roof on my outdoor room that had stayed in place as I lay immobilised with my incantations for the earth's movements to be arrested. I welled up with gratitude as I lay motionless in the pine circle looking to the skies as the stars disappeared and the dawn orange tinges rose. Mini tremors startled those dozing in and out of slumber, and in those moments only a sharp intake of breath could be heard.

My mind was asking lots of questions that no one could answer at that point. After two days, there was a chill in my own inner thoughts as I had still not heard anything from my partner who was on a nearby island waiting for me to join him in a couple of weeks' time. No phones yet, no messages out or into the centre office, and I started to wonder if he was well. My angst escalated when I heard that the earthquake originated between our two islands and that there had been damage in Skiathos also.

One of the managers returned from an across island trip and we heard more. The village news was that a sticky golden elixir, melded with many liquors, was running down the cobbled streets as the honey shop shelves had fallen down and some bars had disintegrated. I could inhale the aroma of that mess. There were reports of cars being smashed by huge stones falling off buildings, and rolling rocks tumbling from the pinnacle where the church is perched at the top of the island. Thankfully there were no serious injuries.

I believe that when unusual things happen, they are messages for us. The earthquake had really loosened my roots and I realised that I actually had very few of those to secure me. At this point, I had been living between Edinburgh and the Scottish Highlands for some time, with most of my everyday needs stored permanently in my car. As the non-communicative days passed, my roots were weakened and it was time for me to address that. I had to vote with my feet and find stronger stable ground on which to move forward. This meant less travelling around and more being in one place, creating foundations on which my relationship could grow. Amidst my pondering on selling my city home, moving to the Highlands, changing my work pattern, and generally uprooting myself completely and planting myself elsewhere, I had a very clear visual image. It was of the earthquake happening between my partner and I as a reminder of the fragility of the Earth and how precious our time is here on our planet. Neither of us had been making the most of that and we were both living in limbo, unprepared to uproot and move. I have often mustered the courage to let go of the good in order to make space for the great, so my plan was now formulating nicely, the hinging factor being that my partner was safe on his island and perhaps having something of a reality check too. It felt like a long time not to know about his wellbeing and it passed slowly with occasional flutters of panic that needed to be quelled.

As the new moon was birthed, we were reunited on the bustling harbour of Skiathos town. It was an emotional meeting of eight limbs and two souls entangling, and I felt it was time for that to be happening on a more regular basis.

It was not until I had a glimpse of my life without a significant person in it that I realised the need for positive action to move my life in a different direction. Thankfully my hatching plan was met a with a favourable response and much chatter ensued about how the next weeks, months, and years might map out. I truly believe that without a literal earth-moving experience, we would have bumbled along without a sense of belonging for many more moons. It served me well, although I hope not to repeat such a dramatic experience to sharpen my awareness of checking in with myself and taking a more scrupulous view below and above the surface. Since that trip I encourage myself to build strong self roots, so that wherever I am I can feel their resilience to be proactive and cope with change when it is needed on my soul journey.

I reflect on these experiences and while my two episodes may seem loosely connected, for me they are inextricably intertwined. Positive intention speaks to me of having focus, purpose, and a clear vision of creating something that attracts goodness into time and space. Those caring and loving hands that held nurturing moments for an acquaintance were a poignant reminder of how simple it is to be fully present with positive intention and that this is always enough. It is up to the recipient what they choose to embrace. The earthquake similarly pulled me into the now, allowing me to recognise that wherever I go, whatever I do, I can choose to be strongly earthed, rooted, and fully present with all of my heart. Again I observe that those on the journey with me can decide how much they wish to engage and my open and ever present heart is most certainly, always enough.

Jude lives and works as a therapist and artist in a small Scottish Highland village. She enjoys being active in her local community, walking in the stunning surroundings, cycling, and tending her cottage garden.

Mia Middleton

Awakening to the Wonder of Us

A Misfit. That is how it felt to be in this world from a very young age, but what I have come to realise is that we are all misfits rediscovering the wonder that is us.

The first recollection I have of the spirit world was as a young child. I can't quite remember the age but I was still young enough to have the incredible power of imagination, wonder, and joy, that is a child's innate magic. How have adults come to rationalise their child's creative intuitive powers? As 'imaginary friends.' As 'night terrors' and 'making up stories.' Sometimes even lies. How soul-destroying to hear parents and influential figures crush the fertile creativeness of a child by telling them they are liars. Unfortunately, this is how we often label a source of pure and unfettered knowledge that is only now starting to gain more understanding.

With an awakening and acknowledgement of the continuation of life, we are coming to realise that if we nurture the pure soul essence that we come into this world with, free from judgement, societal rules, and cultural agendas, the innate understanding of the connectedness of all that there is can heal this world.

Like all young children, my mind had the ability to see past the material 'reality' our adult minds are reduced to when societal expectations close the door on dreams that were once bursting with untapped potential. Figures and impressions we call ghosts would visit me at night. How utterly terrifying for a child. The figures were as solid and physical as we see in our everyday lives. Lying alone in a dark bedroom when all was silent, and a dark figure walks through the door and stands at the base of your bed to talk to you, is not a fun and joyful experience, especially when all the ghost stories you've heard don't end up well. Numerous times my mother was woken up to me either shouting or knocking on her bedroom door to say there is a man or woman in my room talking to me and asking me stuff. Mum put this down to sleep walking and night terrors and so she would stay beside me or I would go and sleep in her bed.

One day we were walking down to the beach on a beautiful sunny day, when I stopped to speak to an old couple standing at the top of the cliffs. They were telling me about someone in our village and how life was treating this particular woman. I don't remember talking back to them, but I do remember Mum calling on me and telling me to hurry up as I was lagging behind. I said to her, *I was just talking to the couple sitting on the seat at the top of the cliffs* and she said, *what couple?* That was the only time I remember ever seeing spirits in broad daylight. From then on, my sixth sense disappeared, or seemed to. It was very confusing. I think the impetus for the disappearance was a scary incident one night when a tall dark figure came to me and stood at my bedroom door. I knew he was not bringing me good news. I screamed and asked him to leave. My mother ran into my room worried about what was happening to me, so my mind shut it all down.

I grew up still feeling like a misfit and I suppose that was always going to be an inevitable part of being a mixed-race child of a single parent in the north-east of Scotland in the 70s, having moved from bustling, multi-cultural London. I was the only dark-skinned (I would say more of a latte colour myself but the kids called me black) child in about a sixty mile radius.

Mine was not an easy life. When you are a medium, in between worlds, the next door you open will always make you remember who you are, no matter how far the expectations of this world may encourage you to veer off. It's one of the most wonderful phenomena of this life. I believe we are all mediums. Some have been fortunate enough to be born in homes and groups that are already awakened to the preciousness of a child's soul. They protect the natural evolution of the child's awakening, understanding the needs of a vulnerable life. These children question the way we live – they question and explore everything and are free to express the genius in their soul. We must ask them what they think, rather than shut them down or tell them *that's the way it's always been* or *don't do it like that, do it like this!* Look where that attitude got us.

The re-awakening of my connection to spirit has taken time to rouse from its deep slumber. It felt like I was living in a tomb for most of my early adulthood. My only parental support was an emotionally unavailable and unreachable mother, due to her own disintegrated shadow. I was scrambling around in the dark trying to live a life that never seemed to get off the ground because there was no light showing me a way out. The chinks of light that were squeezing through the cracks from the brief interactions with concerned and well-meaning adults, just made the environment appear foggy and jumbled. I was too scared to move. What lay ahead? With very low confidence and self-esteem, my creative potential was lifeless and I was at the mercy of unscrupulous individuals with their own self-centred agendas whose views and opinions I felt must be more important than my own. So I became something else to try to fit in.

Layer upon layer of other people's expectations, judgements, and opinions covered my soul, until the weight became so stifling that one day, I felt that I could not get up off the ground, and I told God I was coming back home. God had other plans and sent an angel of the most brilliant spring green light to materialise above my bed as I lay on my sodden wet pillow from yet another night of sorrowful frustrated tears. I was blind to a way out. This apparition started as a vague mist of pale green slowly creeping across my ceiling, a bit like the first signs of a car's headlights catching the top edges of the curtain on your bedroom window as it turns into your street at night. This was no car headlight or streetlight though. Within seconds, this ever-brightening light started to take a form. First there was the shape of a head, then broad ill-defined shoulders, and then strange flaring streaks of light, as if the body was too large to fit the environment it was in. I was gripped by fear and pulled the duvet over my head. How on earth was a duvet going to protect me from something other-worldly? I pulled the duvet back and berated myself for being a coward. I felt a fuzzy bright light surround me that felt eternally healing and reassuring. The message was to let go of where I was in my life and God would help me. The next day at work, I knew I had to write my resignation as a social worker. I had been so stressed, and living a life that did not resonate with me anymore. I didn't know how I would survive but something told me I was going to be okay.

I had had spiritual visits previously but never as clear as that. I had seen the usual symbols we all know as universal signs of a spirit visit: white feathers, robins, triple number sequences. I had heard people walk about my house, up and down the stairs and closing doors. I even had the incredible joy of my grandfather, who'd passed away many years before, speaking clearly into my ear saying, *don't worry lass, you've just won £10 off the lottery.* It was one Saturday morning when I was feeling very low and close to giving up. I got up to make a cup of tea and as I walked slowly down my spiral staircase, I felt a slight pressure in the air close to me and then the most beautiful sound I could ever have wished for, my wonderful grandfather's voice. Have you ever felt so much excitement that your whole insides feel as if they will just burst out of your skin? Tears of love and joy rolled down my face; I could hardly believe what had happened. I couldn't speak, I couldn't move, I never wanted that moment to end. I wanted to hear more but I also wanted to know if what I heard was true. I rushed to find my lottery ticket and check the numbers. I had won £10.

One of the ways Spirit tries to get your attention when they need you to remember who you are and know you are always loved, is via symbols, feeling the air pressure and temperature suddenly change around you, or most commonly at night time in your dreams so that you don't feel so freaked out and scared. I dream a lot about spirit. The spirit world has directed people to me again and again, to pass on messages from loved ones who have passed over, to remind us that we are not randomly placed on this planet and that only when you have completed the mission your soul decided it wanted to learn in this lifetime, will you return home.

This is one of the most incredible journeys I have been on and I now understand that all the pain and challenges I have endured have been to help me fulfil the mission that we are all here to fulfil, and that is to remember and awaken to the wonder that is us.

Mia Middleton is an Alternative Therapist living in Scotland. Originating from an unconventional, mixed race background, Mia describes herself as grounded but hauntingly broken, impulsive and unapologetic.

Angela Mitchell

Ecclesias

Take me to church, as the song says. Or maybe not. As a child growing up in an industrial town in Lanarkshire, I had a baptism of fire in terms of church worship. My father was strict, almost to the extent of Victorian, when it came to morals, manners, and how to treat people. I remember being taken along to join the church girls group, called The Guildry, at six or seven years old At first it seemed okay. I liked one of the leaders – she was one of our neighbours and was a very friendly and approachable lady. So I settled in. However, during one session we were asked to colour in a picture of Jesus. I took a black crayon and scribbled all over the image. At the end we were all to display our efforts and I felt so embarrassed at what I had done. The leader looked somewhat shocked but bemused. She never said anything, well, to me anyway.

Mum and Dad took me to church fairly regularly in those days. I had a feeling they weren't quite as into it as some of the other church goers. I heard my dad say once *what's the point in going, it's all an excuse to get dressed up for what?*

I had been christened, but I wasn't really into God. My father's feelings affected me. He thought it was a hypocrisy.

All the monied folk getting their fancy gear on, on a Sunday. *It's God after all. He's not judging us by the way we wear hats.* Then one Sunday, an extraordinary thing happened. My cousin and I went along with our parents. Our uncle was an elder in the church, and at the end of the sermon bibles were given to the children. My cousin was given hers, but when it came to me, he actually moaned that I shouldn't get it. My parents gently argued, why not? *She's attended the church.* But no, I wasn't to get it. I felt so sad and unliked, and when I think about it, it still upsets me. The actions of adults can be recalled by children. This made me decide that I didn't want to go back to church where adults were supposed to act godly and non-judgemental. Hypocrisy indeed! After that experience, my parents and I stopped attending church.

Fast forward years later and continuing debates between my dad and my visiting aunt from England who had polar opposite views on religion. Aunt Pat, a teacher in biology, believed we came from animals. My dad did not agree. I was left to decide which route I would follow. Being interested in science myself, I followed Aunt Pat's views.

There was one positive church experience I did have. On holiday in Fife, when I was around eight, I went to a church service with my cousins who were roughly the same age as me. I remember really well how fun it was. It seemed a very forward-thinking church with modern songs and fun activities arranged for us too. I thought, wow, if only our church had been like this. I'm not sure though if it would have influenced my thoughts on being a Christian.

When I met my husband, his family were heavily involved in the church. I started attending for Christmas Eve, and when the children arrived, for occasional Sunday sermons and when they went to Sunday school. They were never christened; it just happened that way.

For a period of time, I suffered with mental illness. It scared me and I was worried about it affecting the family. The minister visited me and I actually said prayers. I wondered why I had; I felt I needed to. At the same time though, I felt annoyed. Was there anything wrong with being a part time worshipper? My atheist tendencies were tested. They still are to be honest. I don't attend church now and my girls don't either. I haven't forced my opinion on them, and neither have their grandparents although they still attend.

A few years after they were born, I went to a psychic evening. My father had passed and I went for some soul searching. I was told that his presence was near, the psychic correctly pointed out that Dad had problems with his legs before he passed. Also, that he knew that I felt there was a presence in my new home. I hadn't told anyone that.

It's human nature to believe in something after life here ends. It can't be just nothing? I do believe we go on in some way, just not into Jesus's house. Or the pearly gates.

I had an experience recently where I awoke suddenly – something had touched my finger as my arm lay on the bed. It was a heavy pressure on my middle finger. For some reason I dwelt on this. Was I asleep? Did I imagine it? There were reminders of an experience I had during an Indian head massage workshop. The tutor, a very interesting woman who had found a different path in life, encouraged us to close our eyes and call on our guardian angel. Mine was, bizarrely, my first dog, Glen. He was leading me through the garden of my house and everything was in vivid pink.

The tutor asked us all to share. I was slightly embarrassed to say it was a dog but once I told her the story it seemed right, and someone else in the room had a spirit animal in her vision too.

I've always had signs, but at the same time the science side of me tries to explain them away. One of the best signs I experienced was when Neil and I frequented a popular Italian restaurant in town. We ate our meal then asked for the bill. Curiously it said at the bottom 'two babies.' I looked at Neil and said maybe that means two baby chams? Which anyway we hadn't ordered. We were stumped but Neil had the bill corrected.

What happened a few years later? I had twins! My mind went back to that bill. I couldn't believe it. Coincidence? Feathers, dreams, and the like, have all occurred at different times. Fascinating.

Is there a path already destined for us to take? Fate? As humans we cannot exist without some form of hope that we are either not alone or just existing then dying. The comfort of believing in something is within us all, and it takes on many forms throughout the world. Religion brings people together, but at the same time can rip us apart at the seams.

I consider myself broadminded, nevertheless scepticism can step in. I want to immerse myself in joyful thoughts of the more spirited, and take on the journey further. I had another aunt who would say things freely with no care of how others perceived her. As a child she was very inspiring, very open and honest, and told great stories of ghosts, signs, and hidden meanings.

Maybe one day soon I will embrace the fact that I'm more spiritual than I think. I don't attend church much these days.

My girls don't either. The majority who attend are mostly older. I get more satisfaction from other sources. I find comfort in thinking my parents are still with me in some form. The basis of everyone's beliefs lies in the unknown and wanting to be answered. This may never happen. How do we grasp that prospect? To me it's not about attending a building or idolising an image. It's the sense of belonging, sharing, learning, the acts of human interaction. We are united together even though we are different. We need to believe – in what is entirely up to us, be it prayers, chants, or even taking a minute of mindfulness. It all matters. My whole life has been an experience enriched with the thoughts of significant others. And the ultimate pleasure of seeking the truth every day.

Angela lives in Glasgow with her husband and twin girls. She has been a nurse, and now works in the care sector, and is a qualified massage therapist. She loves to go walking with her dog, and writes a health blog.

Morag Simpson

The Conscious Unconsciousness

My first spiritual encounter was when I was four years old. I was the youngest of five siblings, living in a two bedroomed house with Mum and Dad. I would see silhouettes by my bed and they seemed to disperse through the walls. It frightened me a little, but my mum (who was psychic, as was my gran) would make light and say oh *it's only shadows* and *it's okay because Cliff is there* (referring to Cliff Richard and the Shadows), typical Scottish humour.

I had an imaginary friend called Susan, who was part of my family. Mum would set a place at the table for her (bearing in mind it was already a tight squeeze with seven of us), as I would insist that she had tea with us and I would get upset if someone tried to sit where she was seated.

I started school, but was never very academic like my siblings. Mum would say *leave her, she has other gifts*; all the time, the veil between this world and the other becoming denser until it was almost forgotten. Always an extremely sensitive shy child, I went to Sunday School for a few years and loved it.

Fast forward to fourteen, and I became curious about the bible again and decided I was going to read it from front to back. But the stories didn't really sit with me. One of my brothers gave me a book called *Chariot of the Gods* and it gave me an alternative look at creation and the universe, and this was the beginning of opening my mind to all I'd forgotten.

In my thirtiess, I lost my beautiful mum to cancer and my heart was broken. In my anguish, I began praying again, asking if she was okay. I began to have visualisations in my dreams; they were different from my normal dreams. Mum came to me, back to her beautiful self, glowing and smiling. She had been profoundly deaf from an early age and had worn hearing aids for as long as I can remember, but in one of the visitations she said *Morag, look I don't even need hearing aids.*

The brother who'd given me the book learned Reiki and he talked to me about it and became my first teacher. I found it fascinating and wanted to know more but was a little confused by it because I thought this was a route to connect with Mum. In my grief at that time it wasn't what I was looking for, although it was always there, intriguing me.

I had a young family and was working fulltime as a training instructor for a big American company. I was asked to roll out new 'aspiration training.' I was very shy and told my manager *I'm sorry, I can't do this*. He asked me to please give it a go, and he said *Morag I can't ask anyone else to do it. I don't want you to do this because of what you know or don't know – I want you to do this because of who you are as person. You already embrace what this is about.*

I did it and loved it and was asked to roll out another on diversity, which taught me how different people see different things within you, and some people will help raise you while others will belittle you to keep you small. My biggest lesson was to believe in myself.

My brother kept giving me gifts, like crystal chakra wands. They were all beautiful but I had no clue what they were. He would say *you will know what to do with them when the time is right*.

At forty, I worked as an outreach worker helping people get back into employment. I loved helping people develop a better quality of life. One day a lady came to me – a nurse – who had developed allergies to so many things that she was no longer able to continue as a nurse. She still wanted to help heal people and had done Level 1 Reiki and was wanting to go onto Level 2 to become a Reiki practitioner. I asked for a copy of the prospectus as evidence of what we were paying for; as I took the book, she said *I've got two copies, one for you, so you have the details*. And then she said *it's time*.

It was a sign to stop procrastinating, and I booked onto the Level 1 Reiki training. I enjoyed doing it so much and felt myself grow as a person. I wanted to learn more, and I read books and listened to talks from everywhere. I could not quench my thirst for knowledge.

That Christmas, my son bought me a course on psychic development, which then led me to train in Angelic healing and crystal healing. I was then attuned to Reiki 2 by my brother who was now a master.

Soon after, it came to me that this wasn't just an interest I had in my life, this was a way of life. There is so much conditioning placed upon us that we forget that we are spiritual beings first and foremost, and that we are here on the Earth plane for our soul's growth and to show the way for others.

People talk of when their spiritual journey *started*, but I believe our spiritual journey *continued*, as you made your way into this world, and that it is when we become *conscious* of being from source that the magic and miracles happen. We spend years standing on the outside of spirituality, or as I prefer to say 'not conscious of it.' It seems very confusing and difficult, but in actual fact it's so easy. Unlearn all that you have been conditioned to believe, peel back all the layers, and remember that you are a Divine being of light. We know this – we are given signs all through our lives.

I am no longer that shy girl at the back who would rather not be seen. I'm no longer that person who tortures herself with self-limiting beliefs.

It never ceases to amaze me that when the universe wants your attention, it doesn't wait until you are quiet in meditation. It is in constant communication.

I will never forget this sign I was sent. I was part of a phone-in women's circle, and one night I couldn't make the call but had sent my apologies. The next morning, I was doing my usual rushing about to get ready for work, when I saw above a beautiful magenta energy flow down into the right side of my head. It caught me off guard, and as I said *what was that?* I received the words *Mary Magdalene.* As soon as I had a chance, I called the lead from the circle and asked if they had been working with the energy of Mary Magdalene the night before. She replied *yes, why?* When I relayed what had happened, she was ecstatic that although I hadn't been present in the circle, I had still received the connection. So I have an awareness of the energy of Mary Magdalene, and dip in and out of the Divine Feminine, in between being a healing practitioner, running meditation and psychic development groups, and becoming a Reiki master.

I was advised to book a reading with a lady in California who did quantum readings. When I spoke with her, I thought she was getting me mixed up with someone else. She told me of a time long ago in a village close to Nazareth where I was ill and dying. I was saved by Yeshua, with whom I had a connection, and he wanted me to work with him once again. Within a week of having this reading I was invited to attend an Essenes retreat. At the time, I had no idea what or who the Essenes were. It is believed that Yeshua (Jesus) and Mary Magdalene were part of the Essenes. A few weeks after the retreat, I noticed the energy I was working with had changed. It was so different that I asked every Reiki master I knew to experience it and get their feedback. They all felt a difference. Deep within myself I knew what I believed it to be, but my ego mind would not allow me to believe it was this. I asked a friend who was a Mary Magdalene channel if she would allow me to give her healing. Afterwards, she knew exactly what it was I was working with: the mix of the Divine Feminine and the Divine Masculine – Mary Magdalene and Yeshua. From there was birthed *Magdalene Reiki*. I believe this will be more popular in the future as once again the Divine Feminine will be held in high regard. We are going through so many changes today, many of which are bringing to light inequalities that have to change.

My awakening of my consciousness has had highs and lows, but it has made me grateful for many things. Every day the Spirit world amazes me. No matter how much I know, or how much I am still to learn, I am in awe of the universe and its creations.

My story has not finished, and it will not until I ascend from this world into the next. We start from love and end in love. Love is all that matters for love is everything

When we enter this world, the veil is thin.
Our soul incarnated, a new life begins.
As children, we haven't forgotten our link to Divine,
We know without confirmation, without any sign.
We trust in the Magic for we know that it's true,
Our life is colours of every hue.
We carry within us a beautiful light,
Of our creator, shining bright.
But alas as we grow the veil becomes dense,
And life here on Earth makes less sense.
As we conform to the conditioning, no more to resist,
And become part of duality that does exist.
Until one chance meeting, and we're able to see,
And life is once more what it was intended to be.

Morag lives in Dundee, Scotland. She is a reiki master/teacher and intuitive healer incorporating sound, crystal and angelic energies. She runs meditation and psychic development classes and is committed to helping others on their spiritual journey as well as expanding her own.

Monika Piec Halicka

Discovering Self

Over the years, I have grown and developed in so many aspects of my life. I have met many on my path who, like me, were looking for change, love, acceptance, and meaning in life. One of the main themes was learning to nourish and mend my inner child. For years I hoped that someone else would give me all that I hadn't received as a child from my parents that had made me feel incomplete or not good enough. And yet by my late thirties, I still hadn't seen that the only healer for me was myself. That it is only me who can give permission for change in my life, and that it is only me who can let the healing happen. I discovered that there is no other way than to let the Divine guide you, trusting that there is divine timing for everything in your life.

I was afraid of my own power and my own brilliance for so many years. I fooled myself that all those therapies would heal me, like taking a pill or pressing a button and all the pain of lack of acceptance would be gone. Those therapies did their job, of course, but it was the acknowledgement and awareness of the connections – the jigsaw of my life – that brought change.

I couldn't see it for a long time. I took big steps each time I participated in another workshop or gathering, working on my heart space. I don't remember the day when the 'Eureka!' moment appeared, when I realised that there is only one healer and therapist for myself, and that this awareness would allow the change to happiness.

Here is what I discovered as a holistic therapist: everyone is on a journey, and from time to time we all reach milestone moments. These are the moments when we feel stuck in one or more areas of our life. And then many of us will seek help outside of self.

My discovery was that there is no need to push things to the edge. But also there is no point pretending in life, not discovering who you really are, and not questioning why you are here. We have to allow ourselves to reach our full potential.

We all have free will, so we don't have to do anything we don't want to. When I realised this, it meant I could do things the way I felt was right for me, with a pace suitable for me. It was very freeing. I realised that I didn't have to save anyone anymore, just because I know how or because I see a solution they can't. I have a big heart and a big need to save the whole world. Like many, I forget that helping without being asked can be quite damaging. First of all, it might drain your energy and not a lot will be left for you. Second, by pushing change on someone, you can actually make a person go backwards or avoid the change even more because they feel tormented by that pressure.

I realised I don't like to change my opinion about something and I feel uncomfortable when someone is trying to change my point of view, and of course it is the same the other way around. So that led me to the thought that there is no need any more to change others, even if I think they are (what I called before) 'wrong.'

Then 'wrong" disappeared. No one was wrong anymore! They just 'were.' That's it. Just were. Without right or wrong.

Who am I to know and judge what is best for someone else? I have power over myself only. Myself is my only responsibility.

And the other reason why helping without being asked is not helpful: We are all on a journey, and in some way we all committed to coming here to learn, develop, and grow on a spiritual level. If you help someone so that you do things for them instead of them doing them for themselves, you are taking their lesson away. I am not saying that we shouldn't help. It's more about becoming aware of who we really are and what we can do for our own selves first, for our own higher good. And then once we are harmonised and balanced, we can think about doing things for others.

With these discoveries, I came to a point where my role as a therapist was to hold a healing space, or sacred space, which is an unconditional, accepting time of being together. And in that sacred space, my role is to inspire, ask questions, or use techniques from my therapeutic tool box. The most important role is to be a witness for the person I meet, and knowing that answers will come in the silence, when the client quietens their mind and goes within, into their heart space.

This has allowed me to develop a special unconditional divine connection with each client I meet. It took time, to be with it on my own journey to my own self, to understand how others would feel.

I am a spiritual being having human experiences. And I understand now that what I was experiencing was important to grow. And it gave me compassion and understanding for others in same situation.

Inspiration comes when we see that it's possible to go over any obstacle we are facing because we see someone else has done it.

I was always looking for a therapist or teachers I could relate to. But my biggest teacher myself. And it hasn't finished yet; there is always something to learn or improve about yourself.

My intense self-development started when my first child was born. The thing I wanted most was to be a good mother, and an example for her and an inspiration in her life. But when she got eczema and travel sickness and I didn't know how to help her (and of course doctors couldn't solve it either), I didn't feel so much like a good mother then. I had an MA in additional needs teaching, with massage and physio college training, but I felt a failure as a mother because I couldn't help my child to be in perfect health. I started reading a lot of books about the holistic way of seeing the human body. I started making all our food from scratch, even noodles. I quit all chemicals from my household and that was still one of the best benefits to my daughter's well-being over the years, as well as a blessing for me and the biggest motivator.

I was on maternity leave and used this new time to learn something new. I became a facial reflexology therapist. I flew to Poland, my country of origin, with my baby girl. She was just three months old when I was attending the intensive training; my mum was there to help and to bring my daughter to the classroom for breastfeeding every few hours.

I had named my daughter Nadia, only later checking its meaning. It's Russian and means 'hope'. So becoming a mother motivated me to expand in holistic therapies and energy work.

I am grateful for this opportunity to share my path and my thoughts and feelings about my journey. It helped me to express what I've achieved the last ten years. I didn't realise how much it was, and how huge the last decade has been for me. I am truly amazed and moved. It has taught me how we don't appreciate our own efforts, and how we could do this more to unlock our full potential.

Monika is originally from Koszalin, Poland, and now lives in Kilkenny, Ireland, where she works as a preschool teacher. She is a holistic therapist and keen photographer. In her spare time, Monika loves being with her kids, in nature and especially by the sea.

Acknowledgements

This project has taken our authors on an inner journey of soul searching and they have beautifully articulated their sometimes painful memories and feelings.

I'm grateful for their courage in sharing so that others may gain insights into how life plays out in a singular song. No two are the same, although the paradox is that we are all one blessed energy and so when you step up to fulfil your true potential, it affects the whole.

The Universe arranged for Sue Fitzmaurice, editor and publisher, and inspirational artist and Angelic Guide, Swati Nigam, to join our group.

I honour all our contributors and their bravery, and thank everyone involved in the co-creation with Source of this beautiful book.

All profits from the sale of this book will be donated to charity.

Patricia Iris Kerins

Other Titles from Rebel Magic Books

Your Invisible Inheritance ~ Nikki Mackay

Journeys with the Divine Feminine ~ edited by Sue
Fitzmaurice, Foreword by Patricia Iris Kerins

The Accidental Mary Pilgrimage ~ Sue Fitzmaurice

Social Democracy ~ Steven Godby

The Courage Key ~ Stephanie Renaud

REBEL
MAGIC
BOOKS

www.rebelmagicbooks.com